Islamic Creeds

A Selection

Translated by
William Montgomery Watt

EDINBURGH UNIVERSITY PRESS

Edinburgh University Press Ltd
22 George Square, Edinburgh

Set in Linotron Trump Medieval
by Koinonia Ltd, Bury, and
printed in Great Britain
by CPI Antony Rowe, Eastbourne

Transferred to digital print 2007

A CIP record for this book is
available from the British Library

ISBN 0 7486 0513 4 (paper)

Contents

INTRODUCTION

THE CREEDS

Introduction

1

The historical background

The creeds translated in this book, with the exception of the last, came from the main body of the Muslims, usually referred to as Sunnite (Sunnī) Islam. About ninety per cent of the Muslims in the world today are Sunnites, and the other ten per cent are nearly all Shī'ites of three different kinds. Sunnite Islam is thus comparable to the undivided Christian Church of the first ten centuries, but there are also important differences. One is that there is nothing equivalent to the bishops and ecumenical councils of the Church, and thus no body to give creeds an official status such as the Apostles' Creed and the Nicene Creed have in Christendom. The Islamic creeds formulate the beliefs of an individual scholar or of groups of scholars.

This structural difference probably came about because of the very different circumstances in which the early development of the two religions took place. For a century or more, the Christian community consisted of a minority which had separated itself from its neighbours by its religious practice. It was therefore natural for there to be a strong sense of community in each local congregation, and it was found helpful to have a bishop to lead the group and to maintain contact with other local groups. In early Islam, the situation was altogether different. After the Hijra (the migration of Muḥammad from Mecca to Medina), the Muslims were a majority and politically autonomous. Even if later in some of the conquered lands they were for a time a minority, they were still politically supreme. Because the Muslim community had a political structure, no need was felt to have some further structure to deal with purely religious matters. Indeed, Muslims have tended to hold that for them there was no separation between religion and politics.

Nevertheless, the Islamic community did gradually develop ways of dealing with matters of belief. In the course of the first Islamic century, it became customary for those specially interested in their religion to take up a position in a mosque and discuss various questions with any who cared to listen to them. Such persons came to be known as ulema ('ulamā'), that is, scholars or scholar-jurists. From such beginnings, more formal legal and theological schools developed. It should be emphasised that, in Islam, what Westerners would call legal matters take precedence, and that theology tends to be regarded as a subdivision of law. It will be noticed that in the earlier creeds there are many articles which Christians would regard as belonging to religious law and not to theological belief. It is thus inappropriate to use the word 'orthodox' when speaking about Islam, since Muslims are more concerned with right conduct or orthopraxy than with right belief. I therefore speak of mainstream Islam or of the main body of Muslims, and by this mean the Sunnites.

Theological discussions are traced back to the caliphate of ʿAlī (656–61), whom Sunnites consider the fourth of the 'Rightly-guided' (*Rāshidūn*) caliphs. Some Muslims, however, thought that ʿAlī, Muḥammad's cousin and son-in-law, should have been his immediate successor, and that he possessed a degree of charisma. Such persons may be regarded as the first Shīʿites, a term derived from the Arabic *shīʿat ʿAlī*, the party of ʿAlī. Other Muslims, however, were critical of ʿAlī, and some of these 'went out' (*kharajū*) or seceded from his army on one occasion, because they disagreed with certain decisions of his and insisted that 'there is no judgement but God's' (*lā ḥukm illā li'llāh*). By this they meant that decisions on legal and other religious matters should be based on the Qur'ān. Although the name of a large group of early sects, the Khārijites or Khawārij, is based on the action of these people, their insistence on reference to the Qur'ān did in fact become a central principle of Sunnite Islam, for it is opposed to any uncritical following of traditional Arab practice.

In time, the scholars interested in legal questions found that there were numerous points for which the Qur'ān did not set forth any clear principles. To supplement the Qur'ān, they had recourse to the Sunna or standard practice of Muḥammad, and this recourse could be justified by verses in the Qur'ān which stated that he had been given divine wisdom (*ḥikma*) (4.113; cf. 2.151; 3.164; 62.2). The Sunna was known from ḥadīths or anecdotes about something Muḥammad had said or done, and of these there were thousands. (These were formerly called 'traditions', but this is now felt to be ambiguous and the Arabic word is retained.) Because many of the ḥadīths were clear and precise, they were extensively used by the schools of law. It was also realised that ḥadīths could be invented, and steps were taken to establish which were sound and to exclude the false. Eventually, six large collections of sound ḥadīths were given something like canonical status. The jurist al-Shāfiʿī (767–820) formulated a theory of the four roots of law (*uṣūl al-fiqh*) as Qur'ān, Sunna, analogical reasoning (*qiyās*) and consensus (*ijmāʿ*), and all the Sunnite schools accepted the first two.

Although there was no authoritative body in Islam to give official decisions on legal and theological matters, Muslims showed considerable skill in reaching a common mind or consensus in these fields, and this justified al-Shāfiʿī's inclusion of consensus among the roots of law. This consensus also showed itself in the acceptance of four legal schools or rites as equally valid. The word 'rite' is sometimes preferable to 'school' as a translation of the Arabic *madhhab*, since each Muslim has, as it were, to belong to one of these, and personal affairs, such as the division of his estate among his heirs, are decided according to rules of his rite. The four rites are the Ḥanafite, Mālikite, Shāfi'ite and Ḥanbalite, named after Abū Ḥanīfa, Mālik ibn Anas (d. 797), al-Shāfi'ī and Aḥmad ibn-Ḥanbal.

Various events occurred during the first Islamic century which stimulated theological discussion. For a time, a small group of people referred to as Azraqites (Azāriqa) after their leader Ibn al-Azraq asserted the principle that a Muslim who commits a great sin is thereby excluded from the community, and this meant that unless he went elsewhere he would be killed. The Azraqites seem to have lived after the fashion of a nomadic Arab tribe in the desert, so that the exclusion of a great sinner was possible in a way that would not have been possible in a large settled community. The principle is based on the Qur'ānic statement that the great sinner is in Hell, and the Azraqites, regarding themselves as the only true Muslims and the 'people of Paradise', felt that this status was endangered by association with the 'people of Hell'. Later writers on heresies counted the Azraqites as one of the groups forming the Khārijites; but other Khārijites, while accepting that the great sinner was destined for Hell, tried to find less extreme ways of dealing with such people.

There was wide discussion of such problems among others than Khārijites, and in these discussions the term 'postponement' (*irjā'*) came to be used. It was probably originally applied to various political questions, but later it was linked with a Qur'ānic verse (9.106) which stated that the ultimate fate of sinners was 'postponed' for the decision of God; and it was held that meantime other Muslims should treat them as believers. As will be seen from the creeds, the standard Sunnite view was that the great sinner is a believer.

Those who believed in the doctrine of *irjā'* were often called Murji'a or Murji'ites by their opponents (from the participial form), but this was a pejorative appellation very loosely used. When the writer on heresies, al-Shahrastānī (1086–1153), came to write about the Murji'a, he distinguished the Murji'a of the Khārijites and the Murji'a of two other sects from the pure Murji'a; and then, because Abū Ḥanīfa was often called a Murji'ite, he said he belonged to the Murji'a of the Sunna. The conclusion would seem to follow that the believers in 'postponement' did not constitute a cohesive sect but held different views on other matters; and that at least some of them represent a trend which made a significant contribution to later Sunnite doctrine. Because there was no body to decide authoritatively between sound belief and heresy, such terms could be used pejoratively in an imprecise sense in much the same way as British conservatives apply the term 'reds' to any people with left-wing views.

Abū Ḥanīfa (d. 767) was one of a group of legal scholars working in Kufa, and about 737 he became their head. His original mind helped to give definition to their legal principles, so that they came to form a widely accepted legal school or rite, named after him the Ḥanafites. Some of these scholars in Kufa were also interested in theology. It was possibly Abū Ḥanīfa himself who defined faith (*īmān*) as combining the intellectual acceptance of certain doctrines with the public profession of this, but held that works were not a part of faith. Faith was what made a person a believer, a *mu'min*, because *īmān* is the corresponding verbal noun. This conception of faith was strongly opposed at a slightly later date by the Ḥanbalites, who insisted that works were included in it, and that a person's faith could thus increase or decrease according to his works. The Ḥanbalites also criticised the use of some intellectual methods by the Ḥanafites. In the longer Ḥanbalite creed below, the various groups of people denounced as Murji'ites were probably all Ḥanafites.

Another theological point which was discussed during the Umayyad caliphate (661–750) was God's predetermination of all events and of all human actions. There are many statements to this effect in the Qur'ān. The pre-Islamic Arabs had believed that all that happened to them was determined by Time or Fate (*dahr*, *zamān*), and the Qur'ān tended to speak in terms of this belief except that it replaced Time by God. Thus it is stated that God said that 'no misfortune was in the land or in yourselves but what was in a book before We (God) brought it about' (57.22); and Muḥammad is told to say that 'nothing will befall us except what God has written for us' (9.51). The creeds deal at great length with God's predetermination of events and of human acts. To legitimate their rule, the Umayyads claimed (among other things) that the caliphate had been bestowed on them by God; and a writer critical of their policies alleged that they defended unjust actions by saying that they had been predetermined by God.

Among the opponents and critics of Umayyad rule were a number of scholars who are called Qadarites. This term of opprobrium is curious, for in fact they denied God's *qadar* or predetermination and insisted on human freedom, at least to the extent of regarding individuals as responsible for their acts. This again was not a closely-knit sect, because the Qadarites differed in their views on other matters. When the Umayyads were replaced by the ʿAbbāsids in 750, Qadarite doctrine became politically irrelevant since the ʿAbbāsids based their legitimacy more on Shīʿite ideas. Many of the Qadarites, however, seem to have become Muʿtazilites, and these were more of an organised sect. Because the Muʿtazilites believed in human responsibility among other things, some later writers speak of them as Qadarites. Far from being opponents of the caliphs, however, in the first half of the ninth century several Muʿtazilites had prominent positions in the caliphal court and supplied the theological basis for a series of events which came about then.

Towards the end of his reign, the caliph al-Ma'mūn (813–33) set afoot what is known as the Inquisition (*miḥna*). This was the requirement that certain people in public positions, such as judges, should publicly profess their belief that the Qurʾān, while being the Word of God, was created. This was not, as might seem, a piece of theological hair-splitting, but an important political question. The ʿAbbāsid caliphs wanted to be absolute monarchs, and the vaguely Shīʿite ideas used to justify their legitimacy supported this conception of the caliphate. Shīʿism at this period was a fluid set of ideas. It was the Muʿtazilites who produced the arguments for holding that the Qurʾān is created; and the implication was that, if it is created, it is not eternally true and can be overridden by a divinely-inspired caliph. The contrary view, namely that the Qurʾān is the uncreated Word of God, means that it is eternally true and cannot be altered; and from this it follows that the final decision on legal matters should be not in the hands of the caliph but in those of the authorised interpreters of the Qurʾān, that is, the scholar–jurists.

Most of those required to make a public profession of the createdness of the Qurʾān did so. The outstanding exception was Aḥmad ibn Ḥanbal (780–855), a prominent member of a legal school out of which developed the rite named after him. Despite the weak opposition to the policy of the Inquisition, however, it was eventually abandoned about 850, probably because it was failing to achieve an important part of the underlying aim, namely, the healing of rifts within the community. The abandonment of the doctrine of the createdness of the Qurʾān was tantamount to an acceptance of Sunnism as the religion of the caliphate. In all legal matters concerning the relation of the citizens to one another, the final say was left to the scholar-jurists as interpreters of the Qurʾān, even though in foreign policy and military matters the caliphs and governors tended to rely on their own judgement.

Although the main body of Muslims may be said to have become Sunnite at this period, it was only gradually that they found a way of describing this fact. In Muḥammad's time, they were most frequently called the believers (*muʾminūn*), less often the Muslims (*muslimūn*). They might also be called collectively the 'community' (*umma*) or the

People of the Qibla, that is, those facing Mecca in prayer. The shorter Ḥanbalite creed emphasises that it is stating the Sunna which has to be followed. Al-Ashʿarī speaks of those who follow the Ḥadīths and the Sunna. The term 'People of the Ḥadīths' is also used, though it does not occur in the creeds. Al-Ghazālī speaks of the People of the Sunna. Al-Ṭaḥāwī says his creed is that of the People of the Sunna and the Community (*jamāʿa*), but by this he may have meant primarily the Ḥanafītes and may have excluded the Ḥanbalites. Al-Ījī has the same phrase, but by his time it may have had a more general meaning, as may also have been the case with the adjective *sunnī*. By about 1100 AD, there was a considerable degree of mutual recognition by the various groups of Sunnites, and this was supported by the tendency towards consensus already noted.

Although Islam has tended to think of itself as intellectually self-sufficient, many Muslims in the period from 750 to 850 or 900 accepted a measure of Greek thought. This is not altogether surprising since in Iraq before the Muslim conquest there had been a system of Greek higher education, including various sciences, philosophy and above all medicine. This was, of course, a result of the spread of Hellenistic culture in western Asia following the conquests of Alexander the Great in the late fourth century BC. Doubtless some of the converts to Islam in this region had been educated in this way. Apart from these, however, many Muslims became interested in Greek thought. The caliphs were particularly interested in medicine, and until at least 870 had a Christian as court physician. The translation of Greek books into Arabic which had begun earlier was systematically organised by al-Ma'mūn when he established the House of Wisdom (Bayt al-Ḥikma) as a library and translation centre. Eventually, a very large number of Greek scientific and philosophical books were available in Arabic translations. The contact with Greek thought affected Muslim thinking in two ways: it created the new discipline of Kalām, philosophical or rational theology; and it led to the appearance of a distinctive Arabic philosophy, which has an important place in the history of world philosophy.

Abū Ḥanīfa and his followers were known as the People of Reasoned Opinion (*ra'y*), and they also made use of analogical reasoning (*qiyās*), but it is not clear whether they had been influenced by Greek thought. One of the first Muslim scholars to use essentially Greek methods of argument was Ḍirār ibn ʿAmr, who flourished in the decades around the year 800; and, about the same time, these methods were taken up by several of the group of Muʿtazilites. The latter held several heretical views such as the freedom of the human will and the createdness of the Qur'ān, and, as already noted, provided the intellectual basis for the Inquisition. After the abandonment of the Inquisition, the Muʿtazilites ceased to be important, but they maintained a theological school for a century or two. Ḍirār's position was closer to Sunnism, but he was regarded as heretical on some points. Other scholars of mainstream views also adopted Greek methods, but little is known about them. It is this use of Greek methods which created what came to be the discipline of Kalām.

A prominent part – though perhaps not so prominent as was once thought – in the development of Kalām was taken by al-Ashʿarī (873–935). As a young man, he studied in the Muʿtazilite school in Basra, but about the year 900 experienced a kind of conversion and gave up Muʿtazilism for a more or less Ḥanbalite doctrinal position. He did not, however, abandon the Greek methods he had learnt from his Muʿtazilite teacher, but employed these to defend the forms of doctrine he now accepted. The pure Ḥanbalites, of course, would have none of these rational arguments, but al-Ashʿarī seems to have become part of a mainstream group already using them. While his contribution to the formation of the discipline of of Kalām was important, it was probably not unique, but about a century later his name was given to the important school of Kalām which was then flourishing in Baghdad and continued to flourish for many centuries.

The Ashʿarites were not the only *mutakallimūn* or practitioners of Kalām. Many Ḥanafites (though probably not al-Ṭaḥāwī to any extent) were also attracted by Greek methods, and there was a school in Samarqand associated with the name of al-Māturīdī (d. 944). For long however, this probably had no achievements comparable to those of the Ashʿarites. Ashʿarism was taught in various provincial centres as well as in Baghdad, and in the eleventh century there were several important Ashʿarites in Nishapur in eastern Iran. Most Ashʿarites were Shāfiʿite in law, but some were Mālikite and a few were Ḥanafite. The Ḥanbalite legal school was wholly opposed to Kalām.

Apart from those who used Greek methods in theological discussions, there were some Muslims who were more deeply attracted by Greek philosophy and began to write in Arabic on philosophical subjects. The first important figure is al-Kindī (c. 800–70), whose works have been described as producing 'Greek philosophy for Muslims'. In other words, Greek philosophy of a Neoplatonic type was combined with belief in God. A somewhat similar position was taken up by two later philosophers, al-Farābī (c. 875–950) and Ibn Sīnā or Avicenna (980–1037). Avicenna probably marks the heyday of Arabic philosophy, and it may have been declining even before the criticism of it by al-Ghazālī at the end of the eleventh century. The greatest of the philosophers was Ibn Rushd or Averoes (1126–98), who was more of an Aristotelian than a Neoplatonist; but he lived in the Islamic West (Spain and North Africa) where there was little interest in philosophy, and he had no successors. Avicenna and Averroes, however, were philosophers of world class, and when their works were translated into Latin they gave a great stimulus to philosophical thinking in western Europe. For a time, there was a group known as the Latin Averroists. In contrast, there was a continuing interest in philosophy in the Islamic East, chiefly in Imāmite Shī'ite circles, but this tended to merge into theosophy.

Though these philosophers considered themselves Muslims, they produced no short creeds, and some of their views were looked at askance by the theologians who had paid little attention to Greek thought after the first establishment of the discipline of Kalām. In the eleventh century, however, a few theologians felt that the philosophers' views and methods of argument were having an unsettling effect on more educated Muslims; and one of these, al-Ghazālī, decided to take steps to deal with the problem. By private reading, he managed to gain a very full understanding of the philosophy of al-Farābī and Avicenna, and wrote a long and accurate account of their views. On this basis, he proceeded to write a thoroughgoing critique of their views, which he called the *Inconsistency of the Philosophers*. In this, he showed that many of their arguments were far from having the logical precision which they claimed. He called attention to twenty points where he regarded their teaching as contrary to Islam, considering three of these serious, namely: they thought resurrection was restricted to the soul and did not include the body; they held that God knows only universals, not particulars; and they denied the doctrine of creation by asserting the eternity of the world – a view based on the Neoplatonic conception of emanation.

It is difficult to say how far this critique by al-Ghazālī led to the demise of philosophy in the central lands of the caliphate, since it may have been in decline already. The critique of al-Ghazālī by Averroes, called *The Inconsistency of the Inconsistency* was probably little known except in the West. Al-Ghazālī, however, while attacking the philosophers, became an enthusiast for some philosophical disciplines, especially logic, and was responsible for a further injection of Greek thought into Kalām. Some of the results of this can be seen especially in the creed of al-Sanūsī. Many theologians became more interested in the philosophical basis of theology than in the actual doctrines; and it may be asked whether this was beneficial for Islamic theology and did not rather lead to a form of stagnation.

Al-Ghazālī (1058–1111) is someone whom it is difficult to see in proper perspective. His importance has probably been exaggerated in the West. His account of Arabic Neoplatonism was translated into Latin and had some influence. His *Inconsistency* and the critique of it by Averroes were likewise translated. He also wrote a kind of intellectual autobiography called *The Deliverer from Error*, and this makes attractive reading of a sort which appeals to Westerners. As a result, he has until recently been much more studied in the West than any other Muslim theologian. He has also been thought of in the West as essentially a theologian with leanings towards mysticism; but, for his contemporaries and for one or two following generations, he was primarily a professor of jurisprudence.

There has been little study of Islamic theology in the centuries since al-Ghazālī. A vast amount of material for such study exists, still mostly only in manuscripts. Some of the more popular creeds, such as that of al-Ījī (c. 1281–1355), were commented on many times at great length. The creed of Najm al-Dīn al-Nasafī (d. 1115) is an example from the Māturīdite school in the east. The Ashʿarite school seems to have continued in most of the predominantly Islamic lands; and al-Ījī in the east and al-Sanūsī in the west (d. c. 1486) are reckoned as Ashʿarites. As time went on, however, the theologians seem to have continued their practice of Kalām without calling themselves specifically Ashʿarites. It is also important to realise that in later centuries Ḥanbalite theology continued to flourish with its opposition to Kalām, and to show great vitality. Its most important representative was Ibn Taymiyya (1263–1328), but he does not seem to have left any statement of his beliefs sufficiently short for inclusion here. Wahhābite theology, which has an official position in Saudi Arabia, was largely inspired by Ibn Taymiyya.

Finally, a word must be said about the development of Shīʿism. Until about the year 850, it was probably more an attitude of mind than anything else, and people with very different views could be regarded as Shīʿites. They were believers in the autonomy of the ruler, and also in a degree of charisma in the descendants of ʿAlī. Until about 874, there had been some vague recognition of ʿAlī and his descendants as rightful imāms of the Muslims, though there does not seem to have been any serious plotting to overthrow the ʿAbbāsids. Shortly after 874, however, Imāmite Shīʿism was given a more definite form. It was alleged that on the death of the eleventh imām (of the descendants of ʿAlī), on or about 1 January 874, the twelfth imām, his son, had gone into occultation (*ghayba*), was now immortal, and at an appropriate time would return to set everything right in the world. To begin with, this imām had an agent (*wakīl*) who was still in touch with him, but after the death of the fourth agent about 940 all contact was lost, although it was still (and is still) believed that this imām will one day return.

The declaration of the occultation of the twelfth imām was the basis of the Imāmite form of Shīʿsm, also known as Twelver Shīʿism (Ithnā ʿashariyya). It led to a concentration of the hitherto rather fluid body of Shīʿite opinion and gave it a definite set of beliefs, which enabled it to be critical of the caliph and other authorities without being accused of plotting against them. The leaders of the Imāmites were no longer the somewhat incompetent descendants of ʿAlī, but men with considerable political understanding and influence. For some centuries after 940, the Imāmites were uniformly quiescent and lived peaceably intermingled with Sunnites. The creed of ʿAllāma-i-Ḥillī (1250–1325) states the beliefs at this period.

A change came about, however, in 1501, when Shāh Ismāʿīl, who had established his rule over much of Iran, made Imāmism the official religion of his kingdom. Despite changes of dynasty and the expulsion of the last shāh, Imāmite Shīʿism has remained the religion of Iran, and it also has some adherents in other parts of the Islamic world.

The Ismāʿīlites take their name from Ismāʿīl, a son of the sixth imām of the Imāmites, Jaʿfar al-Ṣādiq (d. 765), and claim that he was his father's rightful successor, and not another son, Mūsā, as the Imāmites hold. A distinctive view is that there must be an actual visible imām. From 969 to 1171, an Ismāʿīlite dynasty, the Fāṭimids, ruled Egypt. In the course of history, there have been splits and regrouping. The most important body of Ismāʿīlites today are the followers of the Aga Khan, and for them he is the forty-ninth divinely-inspired imām.

Another body of Shīʿites are the Zaydites, who hold that the true imām is any descendant of ʿAlī's sons al-Ḥasan and al-Ḥusayn who has claimed the imāmate and has a territory over which he rules. For a time, there were one or two small statelets under Zaydite rule. The Zaydites were also active theologically, accepting some Muʿtazilite ideas, and a number of their books have been preserved. They are the smallest section of Shīʿism.

2

Some articles of belief and the relevant terms

FAITH

The word 'faith' has been used to translate the Arabic verbal noun *īmān*, although the corresponding participle *mu'minūn* has been translated 'believers'. The English word 'belief' is not satisfactory because it places too much emphasis on the cognitive aspect, and one cannot speak of 'a faithful'. Essentially, faith is what makes a person a believer, whereas it is the confession of Islam, or else *islām* in the sense of 'submission (to God)', which makes him a Muslim. It is likely that in Muḥammad's lifetime and even afterwards his followers were known as *mu'minūn* rather than *muslimūn*, and so the caliph ʿUmar called himself *amīr al-mu'minīn*, traditionally translated as 'commander of the faithful'. There was some discussion in the theological schools about the relation of *īmān* to *islām*. Sometimes they were held to be identical, but sometimes *islām* was said to be restricted to outward adherence to the religion, while *īmān* indicated a deeper inner commitment; and this view was said to be supported by a passage in the Qur'ān (49.14f.). Both these views are found in the creeds. Some of the earlier discussions are described in my *Formative Period*, pp. 129–36, but the arguments were somewhat confused, and later creeds show little interest in the matter.

The most important division of opinion among the scholars was over what may be called the intellectual and practical aspects of faith. Following Abū Ḥanīfa, the Ḥanafites restricted faith to the intellectual aspect, and said it consisted of 'professing with the tongue, counting true with the mind, and knowing with the heart' (see The Testament of Abū Ḥanīfa (below), §§1, 23). It is further pointed out that the Hypocrites made public profession but did not inwardly believe. The Ḥanafite view is opposed by the Ḥanbalites, followed by al-Ashʿarī and al-Qayrawānī. For them, faith is not merely outward profession along with inward belief, but also external works (A Shorter Ḥanbalite Creed §7; A Longer Ḥanbalite Creed, §1; Al-Ashʿarī, §29). Those who took this view also held that faith increases if a person acts in accordance with God's commands, but decreases if he is disobedient. The Ḥanafites, on the other hand, vigorously maintained that faith neither increases nor decreases; they presumably thought of faith as that which makes a person a member of the believing community, and he is either a member or not a member. The longer Ḥanbalite creed (§1) mentions (as Murji'ite) the view that faith may increase but not decrease; this view was held by the early scholar al-Najjār and others, and may be based on Qur'ānic verses which speak of God 'increasing (people) in faith' (see *Formative Period*, p. 134, note 45).

Many of the early scholars seem to have practised *istithnā'*, which has been translated as 'expressing uncertainty'. What this practice amounts to is that, when someone is asked whether he is a believer, he does not say 'I am a believer' but 'I am a believer, if God wills'. The longer Ḥanbalite creed commends *istithnā'*, but says it is no more than a traditional pious practice and does not indicate actual doubt about one's status as a believer. The Testament of Abū Ḥanīfa (§3), without speaking of *istithnā'*, insists that there is no doubt about a person's faith.

Some of the earlier creeds have a clause to the effect that faith is faith in God, His angels, His books, His messengers, His predetermination of both good and evil, and sometimes various other points. This is a kind of preliminary statement of what the creed will set out in greater detail, and it is not found in the later creeds.

THE SHAHĀDA

The transliterated form Shahāda has been retained for the Islamic profession of faith, namely, that 'there is no deity but God; Muḥammad is the Messenger of God'. I prefer 'deity' to 'god' here because the Arabic *ilāh* is not identical with *Allāh*, 'God', though related to it. When some Muslims give the translation 'there is no god but Allah', they are probably trying to insist that Islam has a distinctive conception of God; but, while their point is sound, this is not a satisfactory way of making it. What Muslims worship is not a conception but a being and this being is usually held to be the God of Abraham, whom Jews and Christians also worship. The conceptions may differ, but they are conceptions of one being. Moreover, there are Arabic-speaking Jews and Christians and these also worship *Allāh*. Al-Sanūsī bases the structure of his creed on the Shahāda, and has a reference to it in §26.

The term commonly applied to Muḥammad by Muslims, *rasūl Allāh*, is translated 'Messenger of God'. In the past, the term 'apostle' has sometimes been used, and its meaning of 'someone sent' is close to the Arabic. Muḥammad's mission, however, is in some respects on a higher level than that of the Christian apostles commonly designated by the word. Muḥammad is also called *nabī*, 'prophet', in Arabic, but this is much less frequently used by Muslims.

THE ONENESS OF GOD

In accordance with the first clause of the Shahāda, the oneness of God is emphasised in all the creeds. It is also asserted that the only unforgivable sin is to 'ascribe partners (*shurakā'*) to God'. The corresponding noun *shirk*, which means the partnering of other supposed deities with God, has been translated 'idolatry' and the participle *mushrikūn* as 'idolaters'. The opposite of *shirk* is *tawḥīd*, which is properly the assertion of the unity of God, but other translations are sometimes more suitable. Its participle *muwaḥḥid* has been translated 'monotheist' (Al-Ghazālī, §23). This last, of course, includes all believers in God.

In some creeds, the oneness and uniqueness of God is elaborated in various ways, and also His otherness from human beings; but this needs no further comment.

A word should be said, however, about the Muslim belief in eternity. The difficulty is that Arabic has no single word to represent 'eternity' and 'eternal' in English, that is, no word to signify what stretches infinitely backwards in time and infinitely forwards. What goes back infinitely is called *azalī* and *qadīm*, which are translated 'existent from eternity' and 'pre-eternal' in this technical sense, though *qadīm* normally means 'ancient'. 'Being from eternity' is used for the corresponding noun *qidam*. What has an infinite future is *abadī* or *bāqi'* with the noun *baqā'* (originally 'remaining'); the translations 'everlasting' and 'existent to eternity' have been used.

It may also be noted at this point that Arabic has no negative prefix to indicate opposites and has to use entirely different words. Thus, for 'existence' it has *wujūd* and *kawn*, but for 'non-existence' *ʿadm*; for 'believer' it has *mu'min* but for 'unbeliever' or 'infidel' *kāfir*; for 'impossibility' it has *istiḥāla* but for 'possibility' *jawāz* or *imkān*, with the participles *jā'iz* and *mumkin*. It is doubtful whether there is any difference between these two, but *mumkin* has been translated '(actually) possible' to show that a different word is being used.

GOD'S ATTRIBUTES AND NAMES

Muslims commonly hold that ninety-nine 'beautiful names' belong to God, mostly derived from the Qurʿān. In fact, even more are found. These are not listed in the creeds, though al-Ghazālī wrote a book about them. The theologians, however, did spend some time discussing the attributes of God. Al-Sanūsī (§§4, 5) makes an obscure distinction between 'attributes of forms' and 'attributes pertaining to forms' (*ṣifāt al-maʿānī, ṣifāt maʿnawiyya*); the former are expressed by nouns such as 'power' and 'sight' and the latter by the corresponding adjectives 'powerful' and 'seeing'. The translation 'attribute' has here been retained throughout for *ṣifa*, though in the past 'quality' has sometimes been used. For the corresponding verb *ittaṣafa*, however, instead of a clumsy phrase with 'attribute', the translation 'is characterised by' has been preferred.

The early theologians often singled out seven attributes for special consideration, namely power, knowledge, life, will, hearing, sight and speech; and these are listed in some of the creeds. A difference was sometimes drawn between attributes connected with God's essence (*dhātiyya*) and those connected with His activity (*fiʿliyya*). With regard to the latter, it is insisted that the attribute belonged to God eternally, and not merely after He had exercised the activity; for example, He was a creator before He created the world. A prominent place was given to the attribute al-Razzāq, the provider of the sustenance (*rizq*) which keeps every living thing alive; and it was held that, even when someone eats what is not lawful for him, perhaps because stolen, this is still the sustenance provided for him by God.

Since the attributes were expressed by terms also applicable to human beings, care was taken to maintain the otherness of God from everything human. Early discussions had been about whether the terms were to be understood literally or metaphorically, with the latter word taken in a somewhat rigid sense. It was probably Aḥmad ibn Ḥanbal who tried to break the deadlock by saying they were to be taken *bi-lā kayf*, 'without (asking) how'. In the translations, the term 'amodally' has been coined for this important conception. This is in line with the recognition by Christian thinkers that human language never applies precisely to God, and that he is only 'something like' what we call Him.

GOD'S OMNIPOTENCE AND HUMAN PREDESTINATION

Among the attributes of God is *qudra*, 'power', so that he is *qādir*, 'powerful', and these translations have normally been used, although in English 'omnipotence' and 'almighty' would be more commonly used for what the Muslim scholars meant. God's absolute control of all human life is described in considerable detail in some creeds, and was obviously much discussed by the scholars. The view taken in all the Sunnite creeds may be seen as a rejection of the Muʿtazilite attempt to assert the freedom of the human will. While the pre-Islamic Arabs had been convinced that human life is controlled by an impersonal Time or Fate, mainstream Islam, following the Qur'ān, may be said to have given this role to God. He is held to have predetermined every act of a person's life before he was created. Sometimes these acts are said to be set down on the Preserved Table (*lawḥ maḥfūẓ*), and to have been written there at God's command by the Pen (*qalam*). One of the matters that was specially predetermined was a person's *ajal*, the date of his death; even if a person was murdered, it was at his *ajal*. Similarly, as already noted, a person's *rizq* or sustenance was predetermined.

An attribute of God frequently mentioned in this connection is His *qadar*. The translation 'predetermination' has mostly been used, because the emphasis is on God's activity, whereas the alternative 'predestination' suggests rather the human angle. Along with God's *qadar*, His *qaḍā'* or 'decree' is often mentioned, which amounts to the same thing. It is further held, however, that God not merely predetermines all human activity, but also creates it as it happens. This led to a problem: if God creates the acts, how can they be said to be the person's acts? One answer is that, while God creates the acts, the person 'acquires' (*kasaba*) them. There was much discussion at an early period of 'acquisition' (*kasb*) in this technical sense, but it is seldom mentioned in the creeds. What was widely held, however, was that God creates a human act by creating in the agent the power to act. In ordinary conversation the word *qudra*, 'power', was doubtless used of the human agent, but the theologians carefully avoided it, and spoke instead of the *istiṭā'a* by which the agent was able to perform the act; this word comes from a root meaning 'obey' and has here been translated 'acting-power'. The mainstream theologians further maintained that God created the *istiṭā'a* only at the time of the act, not beforehand.

The modern Western reader sees a further problem here. If a person was bound to perform a sinful act and could not avoid it, why should he be punished? The Muslim theologians, however, firmly believed that, though the acts were predetermined and created by God, they were nevertheless the person's acts. The conception of 'acquisition' or *kasb* had tried to deal with this problem. It was further held, however, that those predestined for a good life were helped by God, receiving His 'succour' (*tawfīq*), so that acts of obedience were easier for them; they were also said to be guided by God. On the other hand, those predestined for an evil life were said to be abandoned by God or led astray. Sometimes, but only sometimes, this succour or abandonment by God seems to follow on a good or bad decision by the person.

Clearly, the mainstream Islamic theologians had failed to produce an intellectual reconciliation of God's omnipotence with human responsibility. The Western Christian may feel that there was too little attempt to maintain in theory some degree of human freedom. Before he becomes too critical of Muslim thinking, however, he should ask whether the Christian West – at least at the popular level, but perhaps also at the theological – has been any more successful in reconciling divine omnipotence with human responsibility, since it would seem to have exaggerated the extent of human freedom, and to have reduced unduly the degree of divine control of human affairs.

THE QUR'ĀN

For Muslims, the Qur'ān is the Speech of God. This means much the same as the English term 'Word of God', except that Speech is also held to be one of God's eternal attributes.

The Sunnite creeds are mainly concerned to assert the uncreatedness of the Qur'ān, and this is part of the basic Sunnite position in opposition to Shī'ite views, as explained above. Because the Qur'ān is uncreated, it is unchangeable, and the only authoritative interpretation of its laws and regulations is that of the recognised scholar-jurists. Whether the Qur'ān is created or uncreated was thus essentially a political question; was the final authority on the divine law an inspired caliph or the body of jurists?

The theologians also spent some time discussing various subordinate points. It was obvious that the Qur'ān was often written down on paper and orally recited; and the ink and paper and the physical sounds were obviously created; but the solutions given to this problem did not affect the main issue of the Sunnite-Shī'ite divide. One of the words commonly used of the reciting of the Qur'ān was 'utterance' (*lafẓ*). There was sometimes also felt to be a problem about how what was eternal could be revealed at a particular point in time; and one suggestion was that what was revealed to Muḥammad was not the eternal Qur'ān itself, but an 'indication' (*dalāla*) of it.

The word *kalām*, besides meaning the Speech of God, is also, as explained above, used for the discipline of philosophical theology, but in this sense the Arabic word has been retained in transliteration – Kalām.

THE PROPHETHOOD OF MUḤAMMAD

The second clause of the Shahāda speaks of Muḥammad as the Messenger of God, but the theologians preferred to think of prophethood rather than messengership. This may be because they regarded prophethood as more inclusive, since all messengers were prophets, but only prophets with a further special call were messengers of God. Following the Qur'ān, the theologians regarded Muḥammad as coming at the end of a long series of prophets. The Qur'ān calls him the 'seal' (*khātam*) of the prophets (33.40); and although to the first hearers this probably only meant that he confirmed previous prophets, by the time of the creeds it was universally interpreted to mean that he was the last of the prophets, after whom there would be no other; and this implies that Muḥammad has the final word of God for humankind. Al-Ghazālī (§15) goes so far as to call him 'the prince of the human race'. Muḥammad was also set above other prophets by his ascension into heaven. This is held to be mentioned in the Qur'ān (17.1), and al-Ṭa-ḥāwī (§9) further identified the occasion with the vision described in Sūra 53.1–12.

God is held to produce evidentiary-miracles (*muʿjizāt*) to confirm that those claiming prophethood are genuinely receiving revelations from Him. These evidentiary-miracles are happenings beyond the normal course of events which cannot be brought about by human beings. From them are distinguished the wonder-miracles (*karamāt*) which God produces to honour 'saints' (the *awliyā'* or 'friends' of God).

As mentioned in some of the creeds, Muslims profess to honour and accept all the previous prophets. Originally, it was supposed that the revelations to these prophets were basically the same as that to Muḥammad, and so were acceptable to Muslims. After a time, however, it came to be realised that there were important differences between the Qur'ān and the Jewish and Christian scriptures; and, in the course of the first Islamic century, Muslim scholars elaborated the view that the Jewish and Christian scriptures were largely corrupt. They based this view on verses in the Qur'ān, but these dealt only with minor matters (*Early Islam*, p. 77f.). Al-Ghazālī is careful to state that the law given to Muḥammad abrogated the laws given to previous prophets except where it explicitly confirmed them; but he accepts the Torah, Psalms and Gospel, though presumably only in their true or uncorrupted form (§10).

While the Qur'ān is the primary scripture for Islam, there is also a secondary type of scripture in the collections of sound ḥadīths from which it is possible to learn the Sunna or standard practice of Muḥammad. Deviation from the principles of the Qur'ān and the Sunna as generally accepted was *bidʿa*, 'innovation', which is tantamount to heresy; the participial noun is *mubtadiʿ*, 'innovator'.

The chief method of determining the soundness of a ḥadīth was to look at its *isnād* (literally 'support'), which was transmitted along with the body of the ḥadīth. The *isnād* was the chain of authorities who had transmitted the anecdote; for example, 'A said that B told him that he had heard from C that Muḥammad once said ...'; and A, B and C had all to be reliable persons. Sometimes there were several satisfactory *isnāds* for the same ḥadīth, sometimes only one. There were also cases where there was no exact *isnād*, but where the anecdote was a matter of common belief, so that it was held to be impossible that the large number of people involved could all have been mistaken; this type of ḥadīth was described as *mutāwatir*, which has been translated as 'widely transmitted'. The creeds do not distinguish as clearly as might have been expected between ḥadīths in the strict sense of anecdotes about Muḥammad and the anecdotes about other Muslims, but use vaguer terms such as 'reports' (*āthār*).

Only recognised scholar-jurists were entitled to state how the general principles found in the Qur'ān and the Sunna were to be applied in practice, and each ordinary Muslim had to follow one such jurist. This was known as *taqlīd* or the following of an authority, and is insisted on in the longer Ḥanbalite creed (§17) in respect of matters of belief.

THE COMPANIONS

The insistence of the creeds that only good is to be spoken of the Companions of Muḥammad is perhaps part of a deliberate attempt to idealise the first quarter-century or so of Islam. 'Companion' is a technical term for all who had seen and known Muḥammad, male and female. In the *isnād* of a ḥadīth, the first reporter must, of course, be a Companion. The names of the Companions and some details about them were carefully preserved, and there are biographical dictionaries of them with 1,000 or more entries. The legitimacy and order of the first four caliphs, Abū Bakr, ʿUmar, ʿUthmān and ʿAlī, who were all Companions, features in the creeds because it is a central point of belief for Sunnite Islam and a rejection of Shīʿite claims.

ESCHATOLOGY

The creeds contain a number of articles about eschatological matters, some of which are at a much more popular level than, say, the discussions of the attributes of God. The starting point is, of course, the Qur'ān, which gives a prominent place to the doctrine of the Last Judgement. The main thought is that on the Last Day or Day of Judgement people will be raised from the dead, brought before God for trial, and assigned to Paradise or Hell according as their actions have been good or evil. The commonly-used terms are *al-janna*, 'the garden', and *al-nār*, 'the fire', for which the translations 'Paradise' and 'Hell' have normally been used. A person's fate is sometimes said to be decided by the book recording his acts (69.19–32; 84.7–12). Sometimes the person's acts are said to be weighed in a balance (101.6–9; 7.8f.). This judgement is the 'reckoning' (*ḥisāb*) mentioned in some of the creeds. Among the delights of Paradise for those assigned to it is the vision of God (75.23). The Qur'ān has no clear statement about Muslim sinners being released from Hell after a time, but it does speak of the possibility of intercession (*shafāʿa*) for them by God's permission

(2.255; 10.3; 19.87; 20.109; 34.23). The Qur'ān does not name Muḥammad as an intercessor, but, as can be seen from the creeds, it came to be generally held that he would intercede for the sinners of his community, and that these would leave Hell after being sufficiently punished.

One of the popular beliefs not mentioned in the Qur'ān is that of the Punishment of the Tomb. The dead were thought to have some sort of consciousness and to suffer punishment for sins; this sometimes followed on interrogation by two superhuman beings, Munkar and Nakīr. The Hour (*sā'a*) is mentioned in the Qur'ān as a variant name for the Last Day, and there are several descriptions of the portents which will herald and accompany it, such as the blast of a trumpet (*ṣūr, nāqūr*) and the disappearance of the world as we know it. The creeds say little about the end of the world, but mention other signs of the Hour (Al-Ṭaḥāwī, §45; Al-Nasafī, §38), such as the coming of the one-eyed Dajjāl (a name derived from a Syriac word meaning 'deceiver'). This was a powerful being who before the coming of the Hour would seduce and tyrannise much of the world, but would be defeated and killed by 'Īsā (Jesus) descended from heaven.

Many of the creeds speak of the Basin and the Bridge. The Bridge (*ṣirāṭ*) is stretched over hell, and is sharper than a sword and finer than a hair. All have to cross it; the wicked fall from it into Hell, but the upright are enabled to cross safely. Then (at least according to Al-Ghazālī, §21) the upright come to the Basin (*ḥawd*), a vast lake of sweet-tasting liquid from which they drink before entering Paradise, and never thirst again.

Just how all these popular ideas relate to the basic Qur'ānic description of the Last Judgement is far from clear, but their mention in the creeds suggests that they were widely believed in by ordinary Muslims.

3

Note on literature

A fuller account of the course of Islamic theology will be found in my book *Islamic Philosophy and Theology* (enlarged edition, Edinburgh University Press, 1985); and a much fuller account of the period up to 950 in my *The Formative Period of Islamic Thought* (Edinburgh University Press, 1973). An important pioneer work was Duncan Black Macdonald's *Development of Muslim Theology, Jurisprudence and Constitutional Theory* (New York, Scribner, 1926); in the Appendix to this volume there are translations of the creeds of al-Ash'arī, al-Ghazālī, al-Nasafī and al-Faḍālī (d. 1821). (Al-Faḍālī was an Egyptian scholar with philosophical interests similar to those of al-Sanūsī, but his creed was too long for inclusion here.) Arent Jan Wensinck's *The Muslim Creed: its Genesis and Historical Development* (Cambridge University Press, 1932) contains translations of three Ḥanafite creeds and summaries of some others, while the commentaries on these draw on his incomparable knowledge of the ḥadīth literature.

For Ḥanbalism, there is the seminal work of Henri Laoust, *Essai sur les doctrines sociales et politiques de Taḳī-d-dīn Aḥmad b. Taimīya* (Cairo, Institut Français d'Archéologie Orientale, 1939), referred to as *Ibn Taimīya*. This is supplemented by his *La Profession de foi d'Ibn Baṭṭa* (Damascus, Institut Français, 1958).

English translations are available of some longer statements of Shī'ite belief. For the Imāmites, there is *A Shī'ite Creed* by Asaf A. A. Fyzee (London, Oxford University Press, 1942) and *Shī'ite Islam* by 'Allāmah ... Ṭabāṭabā'ī, translated and edited by Seyyid Hossein Nasr (London, George Allen and Unwin, 1975. For the Ismā'īlites, there are two translations by W. Ivanow: *A Creed of the Fatimids* (Bombay, Qayyimah Press, 1936) and *True Meaning of Religion* by Shihābu' d-dīn Shah al-Ḥuseyni (Bombay, 1933).

Other works referred to in the notes are:

Watt, W. M., *Muhammad's Mecca: History in the Quran* (Edinburgh University Press, 1988).

Watt, W. M., *Early Islam: Collected Articles* (Edinburgh University Press, 1991).

4

Standard translations

In the creeds, the aim has been to keep to the same English word for each Arabic technical term, and the chief standard translations are given here. Occasionally one of these may have seemed unsuitable in a particular context, and a few slips may have been made. Brackets have been put round words for which there is no Arabic word, though the idea is implied. Ascriptions of praise have been omitted. A hyphen has sometimes been used to show that two English words translated one Arabic word.

abadī existing to eternity, everlasting
ʿabd human being; but *ʿabdu-hu* His servant
ʿadm non-existence
ajal appointed term
ʿaraḍ, plural *aʿrāḍ* accident(s)
ʿarsh throne
athar reported saying, report
azalī existent from eternity, pre-eternal

baqāʾ being to eternity; adjective *bāqiʾ*
bidaʿ innovation

dhāt essence

fanāʾ passing away
fardaniyya uniqueness
faḍīla supererogatory
faḍl grace
farīḍa obligatory

ḥādith originated; noun *ḥudūth* origination
ḥaqīqa real nature
ḥawḍ basin
ḥisāb reckoning

ʿibād human beings
ījād bringing into being
ilhām inspiration
īmān faith

irāda will
istighnā' independence
istiḥāla impossibility
istiṭā'a acting-power
istithnā' expression of uncertainty
ittaṣafa characterised by

jā'iz possible; noun *jawāz* possibility
jawhar atom

kāfir unbeliever; noun *kufr* unbelief
kā'ina entity
kalām speech; but as philosophical theology is transliterated Kalām
khālidūn everlastingly
karamāt wonder-miracles
kursī sedile

lawḥ maḥfūẓ preserved table

ma'ād return
maḥall place
maḥāll impossible
ma'nā, ma'ānī form(s) or meaning(s)
maṣāḥif copies
mashī'a will, volition
mawjūd existent (thing)
mīthāq pledge
muḥāsiba settling of accounts, reckoning
mu'jizāt evidentiary-miracles
mukallaf mature believer
mukhaṣṣiṣ determinant
mu'min believer
mumkin actually-possible
murakkab composite
mustaḥīl impossible
mutawātir widely transmitted

qaḍā' decree
qadar predetermination, predestination
qadīm pre-eternal, existent from eternity; noun *qidam*
qiyām bi-nafsi-hi self-subsistence
qiyās analogical reasoning

ra'y reasoned opinion
rāziq sustainer, (provider of sustenance – *rizq*)

ṣalāt formal worship
ṣamad enduring
shafā'a intercession
shar' revelation
shirk idolatry
ṣifa attribute

taklīf imposition of duties
tanzīh purity of conception
taqdīr determination
taqlīd following an authority
tashbīh anthropomorphism
tawfīq succour
ta'ṭīl denial (of attributes)
tawḥīd assertion of oneness

waḥdāniyya unicity
waḥy revelation
wājib necessary; *noun wujūb*

zindīq dualist

The Creeds

The Ḥanbalites

The career of Aḥmad ibn Ḥanbal (780–855) has been described in the Introduction, and something has been said about the distinctive anti-rationalist theological position of his followers. In *La Profession de foi d'Ibn Baṭṭa* (Damascus, 1958) Henry Laoust called attention to six Ḥanbalite creeds which are reproduced in *Ṭabaqāt al-Ḥanābila* by Ibn Abī Yaʿlā (also known as Abū l-Ḥusayn ibn al-Farrā') (Cairo 1952). These creeds are incorporated in biographical notices of members of the school, most of whom are very obscure persons. Three are translated here, called by Laoust ʿAqīda V, II and I respectively. At a few points (indicated by ellipses), there have been brief omissions of difficult statements which did not seem to add anything to what was being asserted.

The first creed here may contain the actual words of Aḥmad ibn Ḥanbal, since it occurs in the notice of Abū Jaʿfar Muḥammad ibn ʿAwf, who claims that Aḥmad dictated it to him (*Ṭabaqāt*, i 311–3). Much of it deals with eschatological matters. The uncreatedness of the Qur'ān is asserted, but there is no mention of the discussions about the 'utterance' (*lafẓ*) of the Qur'ān. It is insisted that faith (being a believer) includes actions as well as verbal profession, and may increase and decrease; this is the distinctive Ḥanbalite position in contrast to the Ḥanafites.

The short creed which follows (*Ṭabaqāt*, i 130f.) is primarily concerned with the practice of religion and not with belief about God.

The longer creed (*Ṭabaqāt*, i 24–31) was translated in abbreviated form in my *Formative Period* (pp. 292–4). While the assertions of this creed are much the same as those of the other two, there are one or two points which suggest that it may have taken shape at a later date: it gives a fuller account of the discussions about the uncreatedness of the Qur'ān; it has a more elaborate treatment of God's knowledge, power and other attributes; and it includes the specific rejection of two features of Ḥanafite methods, analogical reasoning (*qiyās*) and reasoned opinion (*ra'y*).

The Ḥanbalite use of the names of sects has been mentioned above, and should be carefully noted. In the case of names such as Muʿtazila and Khawārij, the Ḥanbalites are in accord with standard Sunnite usage, as found in writers like al-Shahrastānī.

They use 'Murji'ite', however, for many different views held by Abū Ḥanīfa and various groups of his followers. The early Ḥanbalites regarded all these views as heretical, but that was not the position of the main body of Sunnites, for whom Abū Ḥanīfa could obviously not be a heretic. The names 'Jahmiyya' and 'Jahmite' are used by Ḥanbalites for persons believing in the createdness of the Qur'ān, but there was no clearly defined sect of this name, and in other writers such persons are assigned to the Muʿtazila or other sects (*Formative Period*, pp. 131–6, 139–48; EI², art. Djahmiyya).

AḤMAD IBN ḤANBAL

Aḥmad ibn Ḥanbal dictated:

1. A ḥadith has come from the Messenger of God in which he says: 'He who meets God with a sin (unrepented) will of necessity be in Hell; if he repents and does not persist (in the sin), God will repent towards him; and whoever meets God after paying the penalty for that sin in this world, that is his atonement.' A ḥadīth has also come from the Messenger of God: 'If someone meets (God) persisting in his sin and not repenting of it, then his affair is for God (to decide); if He wills, He punishes him, and if He wills, He pardons him, provided he died adhering to Islam and the Sunna. If anyone speaks ill of any of the Companions of the Messenger of God, or detests him for something he has done, or mentions his evil deeds, then he is an innovator, outwith the community until he asks for (God's) mercy on all (the Companions) and until his heart is sound towards them all. Hypocrisy is unbelief in God, that is, to disbelieve in God and to serve other than God, while openly professing Islam; this is like the hypocrites in the lifetime of the Messenger of God; whoever of them openly showed unbelief was killed.' …
2. He (Muḥammad) said: 'When two Muslims encounter one another with swords, (both) the killer and the one killed are in Hell.' He also said: 'The insulting (or wounding) of a Muslim is transgression, and the killing of him is unbelief.' He also said: 'Whoever says to his brother, "O unbeliever", has made the word true of one of them.'
3. These ḥadīths are sound and preserved. We submit to them even if we do not know their interpretation. We do not discuss them or argue about them, and we do not interpret them, but we relate them as they have come (to us). We believe in them and know that they are true, as the Messenger of God said. We accept them and do not reject them.

4. We do not abandon formal worship on behalf of any of the People of the Qibla because of a sin he has committed, small or great, unless he is one of the innovators whom the Prophet put out of Islam, namely the Qadariyya, the Murji'a, the Rāfiḍa and the Jahmiyya. He said: 'Do not perform the formal worship along with them or on their behalf.'
5. In one of the sound ḥadīths about the Messenger of God, it is said: 'The Prophet has seen his Lord.' This is transmitted from the Messenger of God himself. ... Belief in that and counting it true is obligatory.
6. The People of Paradise will see God with the eyes.
7. Human beings have their works weighed; of them are some for whom as compensation sin is not weighed.
8. God speaks to human beings, and there is no interpreter between Him and them.
9. The Messenger of God has a Basin, whose vessels are more in number than the stars in the sky.
10. Belief in the punishment of the tomb and the test of the tomb; the human being is asked about faith and Islam – who is his Lord, what is his religion and who is his prophet? And (belief in) Munkar and Nakīr.
11. Belief in the intercession of the Prophet for a (group of) people being brought out of Hell, and in the intercession of the intercessors.
12. Paradise and Hell are created. They have already been created, as comes in the report from the Messenger of God: 'I entered Paradise and I saw in it a castle', and: 'I saw al-Kawthar',[1] and: 'I came upon Hell and I saw its people'. He who supposes that (Paradise and Hell) have not been created is counting false the Messenger of God and the Qur'ān; he will be asked to repent, and if he repents, (well and good), but if not he is killed.
13. When there is no intercession remaining for someone, God says, 'I am the most Merciful', and He inserts His hand into Gehenna and takes out from it what only He can reckon; if He wills, He takes them all out. ...
14. We do not place anyone of the People of the Qibla in Paradise or in Hell, except those of whom the Messenger of God bore witness (that they are in) Paradise: Abū Bakr, 'Umar, 'Uthmān, 'Alī, Ṭalḥa, al-Zubayr, 'Abd-al-Raḥmān ibn 'Awf, Sa'd ibn Abī Waqqāṣ, Sa'īd ibn Zayd ibn 'Amr ibn Nufayl.
15. Adam was created in the image of the Merciful,[2] as comes in a report from the Messenger of God transmitted by Ibn 'Umar. ...
16. Belief in the predetermination (by God), (both) of the good and of the evil.

17. Faith is speech and action (or works). It increases and decreases. It decreases where works are few, and increases where they are many.
18. The Qur'ān is the speech of God, uncreated. From wherever it is heard and recited, from that it begins and to that it comes back.
19. The best of the people after the Messenger of God is Abū Bakr, then 'Umar, then 'Uthmān,[3] then 'Alī. I said to (Aḥmad ibn Ḥanbal), 'O Abū 'Abd-Allāh, they say that you are uncertain about 'Uthmān.' He said, 'By God, they lie about me. I related to them the ḥadīth of Ibn 'Umar, "We were placing in order (of excellence) the Companions of the Messenger of God; we say, Abu' Bakr, then 'Umar, then 'Uthmān; and that reached the Prophet, and he did not deny it." The Prophet did not say, "After these do not make distinctions (in merit) between anyone." No-one has any proof in respect of that. He who was uncertain about 'Uthmān and did not place 'Alī fourth was going against the Sunna, O Abū Ja'far.'

A SHORTER ḤANBALITE CREED

The Sunna observed by the Messenger of God up to his death.

1. Approval of the decree of God, submission to His ordering (or command), patience under His judgement, acting in accordance with what He commanded and refraining from what He prohibited.
2. Belief in God's predetermination (both) of what is good and of what is bad.
3. Avoidance of dispute and argument in respect of religion.
4. The moistening of the sandals.[4]
5. The holy war with every caliph, (whether) upright or sinful.
6. Formal worship on behalf of one of the People of the Qibla who has died.
7. Faith is speech and action (or works); it increases by acts of obedience and decreases by acts of disobedience.
8. The Qur'ān is the speech of God, sent down on the heart of His prophet Muḥammad, not created, wherever it is read (or recited).
9. Patience under the standard of the prince, both when he acts justly and when he acts unjustly.
10. We do not take up the sword against commanders, even when they are unjust.
11. We do not declare one who asserts that (God) is one to be an unbeliever, even when he commits great sins.
12. We refrain from discussing what was disputed between the Companions of the Messenger of God.

13. The most excellent of the people after the Messenger of God were Abū Bakr, ʿUmar, ʿUthmān, ʿAli, the son of the uncle of the Messenger of God.
14. The calling for mercy (from God) on the Companions of the Messenger of God, on his children, his wives and his sons-in-law.

This the Sunna which they consider obligatory and submit to; to accept it is guidance, to abandon it is error.

A LONGER ḤANBALITE CREED

1. Faith is speech, action (or works) and intention, and holding to the Sunna. Faith increases and decreases. It is (right) to express uncertainty in respect of faith, but the expression of uncertainty is not (actual) doubt; it is only an old custom among scholars. If a man is asked, 'Are you a believer?', he says, 'I am a believer, if God wills', or, 'I am a believer, I hope', or, 'I believe in God, His angels, His books and His messengers'. He who supposes that faith is speech without works is a Murji'ite. He who supposes that faith is (only) speech and that works are legal matters is a Murji'ite. He who supposes that faith increases but does not decrease has adopted the view of the Murji'ites. He who does not recognise the expression of uncertainty in respect of faith is a Murji'ite. He who supposes that his faith is like the faith of Gabriel, Michael and the angels is a Murji'ite. He who supposes that knowledge (or religious truth) in the heart is beneficial, but does not speak of it (profess it openly), is a Murji'ite.
2. The predetermination of everything (is from God), (both) of the good and the evil, of the little and the much, of what is outward and what is inward, of what is sweet and what is bitter, of what is liked and what is disliked, of what is fine and what is bad, of what is first and what is last. (It is) a decree He has decreed and a predetermination He has predetermined for (human beings). Not one of them opposes God's will or does other than His decree; but all of them come to what He has created them for and fulfil what He has predetermined for them to do. This is justice on His part. Adultery, theft, wine-drinking, homicide, consuming unlawful wealth, idolatry and all sins (come about) by God's decree and predetermination, without any of the creatures having an argument against God, although He has a conclusive argument against His creatures. He is not questioned about what He does, but they are questioned. The knowledge of God is efficacious in respect of His creatures by a volition from Him. He has known the sin of Satan and the others who sin against Him – and He is being sinned

against until the coming of the Hour – and He has created them for that. He knows the obedience of the people of obedience and has created them for that. Everyone does what he was created to do, and comes to what was decreed for him and known about him. Not one of them opposes God's predetermination and His will. God is the doer of what He decides on and the accomplisher of what He wills. If anyone supposes that for His servants who sin against Him God wills good and obedience, and that the human beings will for themselves evil and sin and carry out what they have willed, then (that person) has supposed that the will of human beings is more effective than the will of God. And what is a greater lie against God than this?

If anyone supposes that adultery is not by predetermination, he is asked, 'Do you see this woman, pregnant as a result of adultery and producing a child? – did God will that He should create this child, or was it established in His previous knowledge?' If he says, 'No', he has supposed that along with God there is (another) creator, and this is pure idolatry.

If anyone supposes that stealing, wine-drinking and consuming unlawful wealth are not by (God's) decree and predetermination, he is supposing that this person is powerful enough to be able to consume the sustenance of another (person), and this is pure Magian doctrine. On the contrary, a (person) eats his (own) sustenance, and God has decreed that he should eat it in the way in which he eats (sc. lawful or unlawful).

If anyone supposes that killing a person is not by (God's) will in His creating (of those involved), he is supposing that the one killed died at other than his appointed term; and what unbelief is clearer than this? On the contrary, that (event) was by God's decree and by His will in respect of His creatures and by His arranging for them, and (was) of what came about by His previous knowledge about them. He is justice and truth, and He does what He wills. He who asserts God's knowledge must assert His predetermination and His will (even) of the small and the paltry.

3. We do not bear witness of any of the People of the Qibla that he is in Hell for an evil he has done or a great sin he has committed, unless there is a ḥadīth about that. ... We do not bear witness of any on the People of the Qibla that he is in Paradise for something noble and good he has done unless there is a ḥadīth about that. ...
4. The caliphate is in Quraysh so long as two people remain (alive). It is not (right) for any of the people to contend with them about it, nor to rebel against them. We do not acknowledge the caliphate of any other than (Quraysh) until the coming of the Hour. The Jihād[5]

is valid along with the imāms, whether they act uprightly or sinfully; it is not invalidated either by the evil of the evildoer or by the justice of the just. The Friday worship, the (celebration of the) two feasts and the pilgrimage (are to be observed) with the rulers, even if these are not upright, just and pious. (Various taxes), the legal alms, the land-tax, the tithes and the (proportion of the) booty and spoils are to be paid to the commanders, whether they have dealt justly or evilly in respect of them. Him to whom God has entrusted your affairs is to be followed, and you are not to withdraw your hand from obeying him nor to rebel against him with the sword, until God makes for you an opening and an exit. Do not rebel against the authority, but listen and obey, and do not break your oath of allegiance. He who does that is an innovator, opposing and separating himself from the community. If the authority commands you to do what is a sin against God, you must certainly not obey him, but it is not for you to rebel against him or to deny him his right. Keeping apart (from both sides) in civil strife is an ancient Sunna whose observance is obligatory. If you are made to suffer, set your self (?life) before your religion. In civil strife, do not give your assistance by hand or tongue, but withhold your hand, your tongue and your sympathy; and God is the Helper.

5. (It is obligatory) to hold back from the People of the Qibla and not declare any of them an unbeliever on account of sin, or exclude him from Islam for some act (of his); but (it is not so) if there is a ḥadīth about that (point) and the ḥadīth has been related as it came (to you?) and you count it true and accept it as it was related, and know that it was as it was related. (This applies in cases of) the omission of formal worship, the drinking of wine and similar things, or where there is an innovation such that the person holding it is assigned to unbelief and exclusion from Islam. Then you follow the report in respect of that and do not go against it.

6. (a) The one-eyed Dajjāl will undoubtedly appear; he is the greatest of liars.

(b) The punishment of the tomb is a reality; a person will be questioned about his religion and his Lord, and about Paradise and Hell. Munkar and Nakīr are a reality; they are the two interrogators of the tomb. We ask God for steadfastness.

(c) The Basin of Muḥammad is a reality; his community will go to drink there; there are vessels with which they will drink from it.

(d) The Bridge is a reality. It is set stretching over Gehenna. People pass over it and Paradise is beyond it. We ask God for safety (in crossing).

(e) The Balance is a reality. In it are weighed good deeds and evil deeds, as God wills they should be weighed.

(f) The Trumpet is a reality. Isrāfīl blows on it and created beings die. Then he blows on it a second blast and they are raised before the Lord of the Worlds for the reckoning and the decree, and reward and punishment, and Paradise and Hell.

(g) The Preserved Table (is a reality). From it the works of human beings are copied (or given their form) because of the determinations and the decree already contained in it.

(h) The Pen is a reality. With it God wrote the determinations of everything and mentioned each explicitly.

7. Intercession on the day of resurrection is a reality. People will intercede for other people so that they do not enter Hell; and people will be taken out of Hell by the intercession of the intercessors. People will be taken out of Hell after entering it and spending in it what (time) God willed; they are then taken out of Hell. (Other) people will be in it everlastingly and for ever. These are the people of idolatry and counting false and denial and unbelief in God. Death will be done away with on the day of resurrection between Paradise and Hell.

8. Paradise and what is in it have already been created, and also Hell and what is in it. God created them and the created beings for them. They will never come to an end, nor what is in them.

If an innovator or a dualist tries to prove (the opposite) by God's word, 'Everything is perishing except His face' (28.88) and similar ambiguous (passages) of the Qur'ān, the (reply) to him is: everything for which God wrote (sc. predetermined) coming to an end and perishing will perish; but Paradise and Hell were created to be eternal, not to come to an end and perish. They belong to the world to come, not to this present world. The black-eyed maidens do not die at the coming of the Hour or at the trumpet-blast or at any time, because God created them for eternity, not to come to an end, and He did not write (predetermine) death for them. Whoever holds a contrary view is an innovator who has deviated from the true path.

9. (God) created seven heavens one above another, and seven earths one below another. Between the highest earth and the lowest heaven was a distance of 500 years, and between any two heavens was a distance of 500 years. There was water above the highest heaven; and the Throne of the Merciful was above the water, and God was on the Throne;[6] and the Sedile was the place of His feet. He knows what is in the seven heavens and earths and what is between them and what is under the ground and what is in the

depths of the seas. (He knows) the sprouting of every plant and tree, of every grain and vegetable, and the falling of every leaf. (He knows) the number of every word, the number of every pebble and grain of sand and of dust, and the weights of the mountains, and the works of human beings and their reports and their breathing. He knows everything, and nothing is hidden from Him. He is on the Throne above the seventh heaven, and beneath Him are veils of light and fire and darkness and what He best knows.

If any innovator and opponent tries to prove (the opposite) by God's words, 'We are nearer to him than his neck vein' (50.16), and 'He is with you wherever you are' (57.4), and 'There is no meeting of three except where He is the fourth ... and He is with them wherever they are' (58.7), and similar ambiguous (passages) of the Qur'ān, then say (in reply to him) that these mean (God's) knowledge; for God is on the Throne above the seventh and highest heaven, and separate from the creatures, but there is no place to which His knowledge does not reach.

God has a Throne, and the Throne has bearers carrying it. God is on the Throne, to which there is no limit; God knows best about its limit.

God is hearing undoubtedly, and seeing undoubtedly. He is knowing and not ignorant, generous and not mean, forbearing and not hasty, remembering and not forgetting, awake and not sleeping, near (with His favour) and not neglectful. He moves and speaks and considers (or observes); He sees and laughs; He rejoices and loves and dislikes; He shows loathing and good pleasure; He is angry and displeased; He is merciful and pardons; He impoverishes and enriches and is inaccessible. He descends every night to the lowest heaven as He wills. 'There is nothing like Him, and He is the hearing and seeing (one)' (42.11). The hearts of human beings are between two of the fingers of the Merciful; He turns them as He wills, and bestows on (or holds back from) them what He wants. He created Adam by His hand in His image.[7] The heavens and the earth on the day of resurrection are in His hand. He places His foot in Hell and it shrinks (?), and by His hand He takes from Hell a group of people. The people of Paradise look on His face and see Him; thus He honours them. He appears in glory to them, and makes gifts to them. Human beings appear before Him on the day of resurrection, and He Himself administers the reckoning; none other than He administers that.

10. The Qur'ān is the Speech of God by which He speaks. It is not created. If anyone supposes the Qur'ān to be created, he is a Jahmite, an unbeliever. If anyone supposes that the Qur'ān is the

Speech of God, but suspends judgement and does not say it is uncreated, this is worse than the view of the previous (person). If anyone supposes that our utterance of (the Qur'ān) or our reciting (or reading) of it is created, while the Qur'ān is the Speech of God, he is a Jahmite. He who does not declare all these people unbelievers is in a similar (position) to them.

11. Visions from God are a reality. When the recipient sees something in a dream which is not a jumble, and tells it to a scholar truthfully, and the scholar interprets it by the correct principle without distortion, then the vision is a reality. In the case of the prophets, the vision was a revelation (from God). What is greater ignorance than to disparage visions and to suppose that they are nothing. ... It has been related from the Prophet that (he said) that 'the vision of the believer is a speech by which the Lord speaks to His servant' and that 'vision is from God'. And in God is our succour.

12. There is a clear, established, obvious, well-known principle that the good qualities (or deeds) of the Companions of the Messenger of God, all of them together, are to be mentioned, and their bad qualities (or deeds) are not to be mentioned, nor the different views about which they disputed. If anyone insults the Companions of the Messenger of God or one of them, or reviles them or criticises them or discloses their defects or shames one of them, he is an innovator and a Rāfiḍite and a wicked opponent. ... On the contrary, to love (the Companions) is a Sunna, and to pray on their behalf is a good work. To imitate them is a means of access (to God), and to accept the reports about them is meritorious.

13. The best of the community after the Prophet is Abū Bakr, after Abū Bakr 'Umar, after 'Umar 'Uthmān, after 'Uthman 'Ali. Some suspended judgement about 'Uthmān. These (four) are the rightly and truly guided caliphs. After these four, the Companions of the Messenger of God are the best of the people. No-one may mention their evil qualities (or deeds) nor accuse one of them of something shameful or of some defect. He who does this must be corrected and punished by the authorities. They may not pardon him, but must punish him and ask him to repent. If he repents, that is accepted from him. If he is fixed (in his false views), his punishment is renewed and he is imprisoned indefinitely, until he dies or goes back (to a correct belief).

14. (The true believer) recognises that the Arabs have rights and excellence and precedence (in Islam), and he loves them.[8] (This is based) on a ḥadīth from the Messenger of God. He said, 'to love them is faith, and to hate them is hypocrisy'. (The believer) does not follow the view of the Shu'ūbites, or the corrupt (ideas) of the

clients who do not love the Arabs, and who do not confess their excellence. Such (persons) are innovators, hypocrites and opponents.

15. He who forbids earnings (or gains) and trading and good forms of wealth is ignorant, erring and foolish. On the contrary, earnings in a (proper) way are lawful. God and His Messenger made them lawful. A man must strive to gain from His Lord's favour (what is needed) for himself and his family. If he does not do that because he does not approve of earning (gain), he is disobedient. Everyone has a right to his (own) wealth which he has inherited or has worked for, or which has been bequeathed to him, or which he has earned – contrary to what opposing theologians hold.
16. Religion is only the book of God, the reported sayings (of early Muslims), the standard practices (*sunan*), and sound narratives from reliable persons about recognised, sound, valid reports (sc. ḥadīth), where these confirm one another. That (all) goes back to the Messenger of God, his companions, the Followers, the Followers of the Followers, and after them the recognised imāms (scholars) who are taken as exemplars holding to the Sunna and keeping to the reported sayings, who do not recognise innovation and are not accused of falsehood or of divergence (? from the true views). They are not upholders of analogical reasoning and reasoned opinion, for analogical reasoning in religion is worthless, and reasoned opinion is the same and worse.[9] The upholders of reasoned opinion and analogical reasoning in religion are innovators and in error, except where there is a reported saying from any of the earlier reliable imāms.
17. If anyone supposes that following an authority is not approved,[10] and that his (own) religion is thus not the following of anyone, this is an immoral view in the sight of God and of His Messenger. (The person) only wants to invalidate the reported sayings, to impair knowledge of the Sunna, and to stand isolated in reasoned opinion, Kalām, innovation and divergence (from received views).

NOTES

1 Al-Kawthar is usually held to be a river of Paradise, and is sometimes regarded as the source of water of the Prophet's Basin.

2 There were ḥadīths in which Muḥammad was reported to have said that God had created Adam in His image, in line with the statements in the book of Genesis (1.27). These are here accepted by the Ḥanbalites. Eventually, however, the majority of Muslim scholars, because of their belief in the absolute otherness of God, rejected the obvious interpretation of such ḥadīths, and found ingenious ways of

making the word 'his' refer to someone other than God (Watt, *Early Islam*, pp. 94–100).

3 Some opponents of the Umayyads held that ʿUthmān was not a true caliph, since he had committed a great sin in not punishing a certain prominent person who had done wrong. Aḥmad here dissociated himself from any such view.

4 It is strange to see this minor point being given much prominence in the creeds, but it was a matter of dispute between the main body of the Sunnites on the one hand and the Khārijites and the Shīʿites. It meant that, in the ablutions preparatory to formal worship (*ṣalāt*), it was sufficient to moisten the sandals instead of washing the feet completely (Wensinck, *Muslim Creed*, p. 158).

5 The Jihād is the 'holy war', although the word itself means only 'expenditure of effort'. Muḥammad was reported to have said, 'I am ordered to make war on people until they say "There is no deity but God"'. This links up with the conception of the world as divided into 'the sphere of Islam' and 'the sphere of war' (*dār al-islām, dār al-ḥarb*), but this conception and the duty of Jihād remained mostly in the background.

6 The Throne on which God is said to be seated is generally *ʿarsh*. The word *kursī* found in this article can mean 'seat' or 'throne', as in the 'Throne Verse' (2.255), but it also frequently means 'footstool'. The translation 'sedile' has been adopted.

7 See note 2 above.

8 Until the end of the Umayyad caliphate in 750, the Arabs were in a special position, since the Muslim community was regarded as a federation of Arab tribes, and non-Arab Muslims had to become clients (*mawālī*) of an Arab tribe. After 750, however, the distinction between and non-Arab gradually faded away. The Shuʿūbite movement was an attempt to uphold the place of the Persian language in the Islamic state (*Formative Period*, p. 172f.).

9 Analogical reasoning (*qiyās*) and reasoned opinion (*raʾy*) were prominent in the methodology of the school of Abū Ḥanīfa. These, and the developed discipline of Kalām, were firmly opposed by the Ḥanbalites.

10 Following an authority (*taqlīd*) was generally regarded as the proper attitude for the ordinary Muslim. He was not supposed to use his own interpretations of texts.

Al-Ash'arī

The place of al-Ash'arī (873)–935) in Islamic theology has been described in the Introduction. Two versions are extant of his creed. One is in his *Maqālāt al-islāmiyyīn*, ed. H. Ritter, Istanbul, 1929–30, pp. 290–7. The other is included in his theological work, *Al-Ibāna 'an uṣūl al-diyāna*, Hyderabad, 1903, pp. 9–13 (English translation by W. C. Klein, New Haven, 1940). The two versions are almost identical, except that one uses 'they' and the other 'we'. The translation here is of the first version, but any significant differences in the second version have been added in square brackets. The similarity with the Ḥanbalite creeds is obvious. The Ḥanbalite critique of rational methods is omitted, but there is no defence of Kalām as such.

1. The sum of what is held by those following the ḥadīths and the Sunna is the confession of God, His angels, His books, His messengers, what has come (as revelation) from God, and what trustworthy (persons) have related from the Messenger of God. They reject nothing of that.
2. God is one deity, unique, eternal; there is no deity except Him; He has not taken to Himself consort or child.
3. Muḥammad is His servant and Messenger, [sent by Him with guidance and the relation of truth].
4. Paradise is a reality and Hell is a reality.
5. The Hour is undoubtedly coming; and God will raise up those who are in the tombs.
6. God is on His Throne; as He said: 'The Merciful on the throne is seated' (20.5).
7. God has two hands, (to be understood) amodally;[1] as He said: '(what) I created with my two hands' (38.75), and: 'Nay, His two hands are spread out (in bounty)' (5.64).
8. God has two eyes, (to be understood) amodally; as He said: 'Which sailed before Our eyes' (54.14).
9. God has a face; as He said: 'the face of your Lord endures, full of majesty and honour' (55.27).
10. The Names of God are not said to be other than God, as the Mu'tazila and the Khawārij affirmed.
11. They assert that God possesses knowledge; as He said: 'He sent it down with His knowledge' (4.166); and 'No female conceives

and brings to birth (a child) except with His knowledge' (35.11).

12. They affirm hearing and sight of God, and do not deny that as do the Mu'tazila.
13. They affirm that God has power; as He said: 'Did they not see that God who created them was mightier than they in power?' (41.15).
14. They hold that on earth there is neither good nor evil except what God wills, and that things come to be by the will of God; as He said: 'But you will not will (anything) unless God wills (it)' (81.29); and, as the Muslims say: 'What God wills comes to be, and what He does not will does not come to be.'
15. They hold that a (person) has no acting-power to do anything before he (actually) does it, and that he is not able to escape God's knowledge or to do a thing which God knows he will not do.
16. They assert that there is no creator except God, that the evil actions of human beings are created by God and the (good) works of human beings are created by God, and that human beings are not able to create anything.

[16a. We hold that there is no creator except God, and that the acts of human beings are created and decreed by God; as He said: 'God has created you and what you do' (37.96); and (we also hold) that human beings are unable to create anything but are themselves created; as he said: 'Is there any creator other than God?' (35.3); and: 'Those to whom they call apart from God created nothing and are themselves created' (16.20); and: 'Is He who creates as he who does not create?' (16.17); and: 'Or were they created from nothing, or are they the creators?' (52.35). This (thought) occurs frequently in the Book of God.]

17. They assert that God helps (or succours) the believers in obeying Him and abandons the unbelievers. He shows favour to the believers, has compassion on them, makes them sound (persons) and guides them, but He does not show favour to the unbelievers or make them sound or guide them. If He made the (latter) sound, they would be sound (indeed), and if He guided them, they would be guided (aright); [as He said: 'He whom God guides is guided (aright), while those whom God sends astray are indeed the losers' (7.178)]. God does have power to make the unbelievers sound and to show favour to them so that they become believers; but He willed not to make the unbelievers sound and not to show favour to them so that they became believers; (on the contrary) He willed that they should be unbelievers as He knew (they would be), and He abandoned them, sent them astray and put a seal on their hearts.

18. (They assert) that good and evil are by God's decree and predetermination; and they believe in God's decree and predetermination (both) of the good and the evil, of the sweet and the bitter.
19. They believe that they do not control (things) beneficial or harmful for themselves except what God wills, as He has said.
20. They commit their affair to God and affirm (their) need of God at all times and (their) want of Him in all circumstances.
21. They hold that the Qur'ān is the speech of God and uncreated; [and that he who holds the creation of the Qur'ān is an unbeliever]. (In respect of) the discussion about suspending judgement (as to whether the Qur'ān is created or not) or about (holding that our) utterance (of the Qur'ān is created), they consider that he who holds the utterance (to be created) or who suspends judgement (on uncreatedness) is an innovator. (Our) utterance of the Qur'ān is not said to be created, nor is it said to be uncreated.
22. They hold that God will be seen by the eyes on the day of resurrection, as the moon is seen on the night when it is full. The believers will see Him [as stated in the ḥadīths related from the Messenger of God], but the unbelievers will not see Him, for they will be veiled from God. God has said: 'Nay, but on that day from their Lord they will be veiled' (83.15). (They hold) that Moses asked God for the vision (of Him) in this life, and that God appeared to the mountain and levelled it, thus informing (Moses) that he would not see Him in this life but would see Him in the life to come.[2]
23. They do not declare any of the people of the Qibla an unbeliever because of a sin which he commits, such as adultery, theft and similar great sins, [as do the Khawārij, who assert that they are thereby unbelievers]. [But (they) do hold that he who commits a great sin, such as adultery, theft and the like, and at the same time declares it permissible and does not believe it to be forbidden, is an unbeliever.]
24. Faith, according to them, is faith in God, His angels, His books, His messengers, and in the predetermination (by God) of (both) the good and the evil, the sweet and the bitter; and (faith) that what missed them could not have hit them and that what hit them could not have missed them. Islam is bearing witness that there is no deity except God, and that Muḥammad is the Messenger of God, in accordance with what has come in the ḥadīths. Islam in their view is other than faith.
25. They assert that God is the changer of hearts, [that hearts are between two of His fingers, as is stated in ḥadīths related from the Messenger of God].

26. They assert the intercession of the Messenger of God, and that it is on behalf of great sinners of his community.
27. (They assert) that the punishment of the tomb (is a reality), that the Basin is a reality, that the Bridge is a reality, that resurrection after death is a reality, that God's reckoning with human beings is a reality, and that the standing before God is a reality.
28. They assert that faith is speech and action (or works), and that it increases and decreases; they do not state that it is (either) created or uncreated.
29. They hold that the Names of God are God.
30. They do not bear witness of Hell (being certain) for any great sinner, nor do they judge that Paradise (is certain) for any monotheist, until it comes about that God has placed them where He willed. They say that the affair of these (people) belongs to God; if He wills, He punishes them, and if He wills, He forgives them.
31. They believe that (by reason of the intercession of the Messenger of God) God will bring out a group of the monotheists from Hell, according to what has been related from the Messenger of God.
32. They disapprove of disputation and quarrelling about religion, of contention over predestination, and of argument over that in their religion about which the disputatious argue and disagree; (that is) because of their (own) acceptance of soundly-related (reports) and of what has come in the accounts related by trustworthy (persons), just (person) from just (person), until (the chain of transmission) ends with the Messenger of God. They do not say 'How?' or 'Why?', because that is innovation.
33. They hold that God did not command evil, but forbade it and commanded good; and that He did not approve of evil, even though He willed it.
34. They recognise the virtue of the predecessors whom God chose for the companionship of His prophet; and they keep (speaking about) their merits, and they refrain from (speaking about) what was disputed between them, (both) the lesser and the greater of them.
35. They set in the foremost (place) Abū Bakr, then 'Umar, then 'Uthmān, then 'Ali; and they assert that these were the rightly and truly guided caliphs, the most excellent of all the people after the Prophet.

[35a. We hold that the imām after the Messenger of God was Abū Bakr al-Ṣiddīq, and that God magnified the religion by him and rendered him victorious over the backsliders, and that the Muslims chose him for the imāmate, just as the Messenger of God had chosen him to lead the formal worship, and that they all called him the 'caliph' of the Messenger of God. After him (the imām was) ʿUmar ibn al-Khaṭṭāb; then ʿUthmān ibn ʿAffān, whose murderers, we hold, killed him unjustly and wrongfully; then ʿAli ibn Abi Ṭālib. These were the imāms after the Messenger of God, and their caliphate was 'the caliphate of prophecy'.]

36. They count true the ḥadiths which have come from the Messenger of God (stating) that God descends to the lowest heaven and says: 'Is there anyone who asks forgiveness?'

37. They hold closely to the Book and the Sunna; as God said: 'And if you dispute about anything, refer it to God and the Messenger' (4.59). They think it proper to follow the ancient imāms of the religion, and not to introduce (as an innovation) into their religion what God has not permitted.

[37a. We rely, in that about which we disagree, on the Book of God, the Sunna of His Prophet, and the Consensus of the Muslims, and what accords with that. We do not introduce any innovation into the religion of God which He has not permitted, nor do we say against God what we do not know.]

38. They assert that God will come on the day of resurrection; as He said: 'And your Lord will come and the angels, rank on rank' (89.22).

39. (They assert) that God draws near to His creation as He wills; as He said: 'For We are nearer to him than his neck vein' (50.16); [and: 'Then he drew near and came down till he was two bow-lengths (distant) or nearer' (53.8f.)].

40. They think it proper (to worship) behind every imām, upright and sinful, on feast-days, Fridays and assemblies; [as it is related that ʿAbd-Allāh ibn ʿUmar used to worship behind al-Ḥajjāj].[3]

41. They affirm the moistening of the sandals as a Sunna, and think it proper (both) at home and on a journey.

42. They affirm the duty of Jihād against the polytheists from the time of God's sending of His Prophet until the last band which fights the Dajjāl and after that.

43. They think it proper to pray for the welfare of the imāms of the Muslims, not to rebel against them with the sword, and not to fight in civil strife; [and to call him erring who approves of rebellion against them when they clearly cease to act uprightly].

44. They count true the appearance of the Dajjāl and the killing of him by ʿĪsā ibn Maryam.

45. They believe in Munkar and Nakīr [and their interrogation of those in the tombs]; in the ascension of Muḥammad to heaven; and in visions during sleep. [We hold that many a vision seen during sleep is genuine, and we acknowledge that it has an interpretation.]

46. (They believe) that prayer for the Muslim dead and (the giving of) alms on their behalf after their death reach them; [and we believe that God benefits them thereby].
47. They think it proper to pray over all who die of the people of the Qibla, both the upright and the sinners, and to accept bequests from them.
48. They assert that Paradise and Hell are (already) created.
49. (They assert) that he who dies dies at his appointed term, and that likewise he who is killed is killed at his appointed term.
50. (They assert) that sustaining (foods) are from God; He gives them, whether lawful or unlawful, as sustenance to human beings.
51. Satan whispers to people, makes them doubt, and renders them mad; [contrary to the view of the Muʿtazila and the Jahmiyya: as God said: 'Those who accept usury will not arise (at the judgement?) except as he arises whom Satan has overthrown by (his) touch' (2.275); and: 'From the evil of the lurking whisperer, who whispers in the hearts of the people, of the jinn and of the people' (114.4–6)].
52. It is impossible for God to mark out the upright by signs which appear for them.
53. The Sunna is not abrogated by the Qur'ān.
54. The treatment of children (who die) is for God (to decide); if He wills, He punishes them, and if He wills, He does to them what He proposes.

[54a. Our view regarding the children of polytheists is that God will kindle a fire for them in the next life, and will then say to them: 'Rush into it blindly', as that has come down in the ḥadīths.]

55. God knows what human beings will do, and has written that that will be; (all) affairs are in the hand of God.

[55a. We assert that God knows what human beings will do, what will become of them, what has been and what will be; and (also) how what will not be would have been if it had been.]

[55b. We believe in obedience to the imāms and in (prudent) counselling of the Muslims.]

56. We think it proper to endure patiently God's judgement, to hold fast to what God has commanded, to refrain from what God has forbidden, to be sincere in (one's) works, and to give good counsel to the Muslims.
57. They practise the worship of God along with the worshippers, the giving of good counsel to the community of the Muslims, the avoiding of great sins, adultery, speaking falsely, showing

factional spirit, boasting, acting insolently, disparaging people, and being unduly proud.

58. They think it proper to shun all those who summon to innovation, to be diligent in reciting the Qur'ān, in writing the reports (such as ḥadīths), and in reflecting on jurisprudence,[4] while (at the same time) being humble, submissive and of good moral character, being generous in well-doing, refraining from (causing) injury, abstaining from backbiting, slander and calumny, and being temperate in food and drink.

This is the sum of what they command and observe and think proper. (For our part) all that we have mentioned of what they hold we (also) hold and formally adopt. We have no succour except God. He is our sufficiency and the best of Guardians. To Him do we call for help, in Him do we trust, and to Him is the (final) return.

NOTES

1 For the meaning of 'amodally', see Introduction, p. 16.

2 What is said here about Moses refers to a Qur'ānic verse (7.143). Moses in Sinai asked to see God, and was told to observe a mountain. God then revealed His glory to the mountain, and it was completely shattered. From this, Moses realised that he could not see God in this life but only in the world to come.

3 'Abd Allāh ibn 'Umar, a son of the caliph 'Umar, was regarded as an exemplary Muslim of his generation. Al-Ḥajjāj was a powerful Umayyad governor in the east, who is here regarded as sharing in the sins and shortcomings of the Umayyads.

4 Diligence in reflecting on legal matters could perhaps be a reference to Kalām. Legal matters include theology, and the word *naẓar*, 'reflecting; or reflective thought', is used in al-Ījī §2 for rational methods in general.

Al-Ṭaḥāwī

Al-Ṭaḥāwī (d. 933) was a Ḥanafite who lived mainly in Egypt. The translation is made from a text of the creed published in Aleppo in 1344/1925. Al-Ṭaḥāwī seems to have been fairly conservative in his views.

The following is an exposition of the creed of the people of the Sunna and the Community according to the school of the jurists of the religious body, Abū Ḥanīfa al-Nu'mān ibn Thābit al-Kūfī, Abū Yūsuf Ya'qūb ibn Ibrāhīm al-Anṣārī and Abū 'Abd-Allāh Muḥammad ibn al-Ḥasan al-Shaybānī. This is what they believe of the fundamental principles of religion and what they observe in serving the Lord of the Worlds.

1. We assert the unity of God, believing by God's succour that God is one. He has no partner; nothing is like Him; nothing resembles him. Nothing renders Him impotent. There is no deity except Him. He is existent from eternity, without beginning; He is enduring to eternity, without end. He does not become non-existent nor cease to exist. Nothing exists except what He wills. Imagination does not reach Him, and understanding does not comprehend Him. He is living, He does not die; upstanding, He does not sleep; creator, without any need; giver of sustenance, without (?receiving) any provision; giver of death, without any fear (of retaliation); restorer to life, without any difficulty. With His attributes He existed always from eternity before His creation (of creatures); by their coming into existence he did not increase in any point that was not previously included among His attributes (sc. He was always Creator). As He was with His attributes from eternity, so He will always be with them to eternity.
2. It is not (merely) since the creating of creatures that He obtained the name of Creator; it is not by His originating of the created world that he obtained the name of World-maker. He has the character of Lordship where there is nothing lorded over, and the character of Creator where there is no created thing. As He is giver of life to the dead (at resurrection) after He has given life (at birth), so He deserves this name (of Life-giver) before His giving of life to them, just as He deserves the name of Creator before His bringing (creatures) into being. That is because He has power over all things, and all things are in need of Him. Every affair is easy for

Him, and He requires nothing. There is nothing like Him, and He is the hearing, the seeing one.

3. He created the creatures by His knowledge, and measured to them their measures. He fixed for them appointed terms (of life). Even before His creating of them, nothing of their acts was hidden from Him; He knew what they would do before He created them. He commanded them to obey Him, and forbade them to disobey Him. All things come about by His power and His volition. People have no volition except what He wills for them. Whatever He wills for them comes about, and whatever He does not will does not come about. Of His grace He guides whom He wills, protects whom He wills (from sin), preserves whom He wills; of His justice He leads astray whom He wills, abandons and tries whom He wills; all of them vary in His will between His grace and His justice. None opposes His decree, none disputes His judgement, none prevails in His affairs. We believe in all that and we are certain that all is from Him.
4. (We assert) that Muḥammad is His chosen servant, His selected prophet, His approved messenger; the seal of the prophets, the imām of the pious, the beloved of the Lord of the Worlds. Every claim to prophethood after his prophethood is deception and vanity. He is the one sent to the generality of the jinn and the entirety of humankind, the one sent with truth and guidance, with light and radiance.
5. (We assert) that the Qur'ān is the Speech of God; it proceeded from Him amodally as words; He sent it down upon His servant by revelation; the believers truly counted it true in accordance with that (description); they were certain that it was truly the Speech of God. It is not created like the speech of the creature. Whoever hears it and considers it human speech is an unbeliever, and God has blamed him and accused him and threatened him with Saqar (Hell), where He said: 'I shall cause him to roast in Saqar' (74.26); and God threatened with Saqar those who said, 'This is nothing but human speech' (74.25). (Because of this) we know and are certain that it is the speech of the Creator of humankind, and that human speech does not resemble it. Whoever attributes to God any of the characteristics belonging to humanity is an unbeliever. Whoever sees this (point and is convinced of it) takes heed, is warned off speaking like the unbelievers, and knows that God with His attributes is not as humanity.
6. The vision (of God) is a reality for the people of Paradise, without comprehension or modality (sc. without our comprehending it or knowing its precise manner). (It is) as the book of God expresses it,

'Faces on that day bright, looking to their Lord' (75.22f.); and the interpretation of this is according to what God intended and knew. Every sound ḥadīth reported from the Messenger of God is as he said, and its meaning is what he intended. We (refrain from) introducing anything (false) into that by interpreting it according to our own ideas or imagining it to be according to our fancies. Only he is safe in his religion who submits to God and His messenger and refers back the knowledge of what is doubtful to the knower of it (sc. does not interpret but admits that only God knows the interpretation).

7. Entry into Islam is established only with outward submission and resignation (of oneself to God). Whoever desires knowledge of what is inaccessible to his knowledge and is not satisfied with the submission of his understanding, is by his desire precluded from sincere confession of the unity of God, from pure knowledge and from sound faith; he wavers between unbelief and belief, between counting true and counting false, between confessing and denying; he is perplexed, bewildered, isolated, lost, neither believing and counting true nor denying and counting false. Belief in the vision (of God) for the people of the House of Peace is not sound in the case of the one who expresses it according to fancy and interprets it by surmise, since to interpret vision and to interpret every characteristic attached to the Lordship (is unbelief and the path of true belief is) to abandon interpretation and to cling to submission (to God). In that is the religion of those sent as messengers (by God).
8. He who does not guard (both) against denial (of God's attributes) and assimilation (of them to human attributes, or anthropomorphism) is mistaken and has not attained purity of conception.[1] For our Lord is characterised by the attributes of oneness and the properties of uniqueness; none of the creation has what is characteristic of Him. God is exalted above limits, ends, elements, members, instruments; the six directions do not comprise Him as they do all creatures.
9. The Ascension of Muḥammad is a reality. The Prophet was taken by night bodily and awake to heaven and then to what (place) on high God willed. God honoured him as He willed and 'revealed to (him) what He revealed; the heart did not count false what it saw' (53.10f.). God blessed him in the latter (future) life and in the former.
10. The Basin, whereby God honoured (Muḥammad) as a source of water for his people, is a reality.
11. The intercession which He has kept in store for them is a reality, as it is narrated in the ḥadīths.

12. The Pledge[2] which God took from Adam and his seed is a reality.
13. God has known eternally the total number of those who will enter paradise and of those who will enter Hell; there will be no increase in that number and no diminution from it. Similarly, (He knows) their acts in that He knows what they will do; and every one has made easy for him that for which he was created. Works are judged by the last ones. The happy person is he whom God's decree makes happy; the miserable person is he who is miserable by God's decree.
14. The principle of predetermination (or predestination) is God's secret in respect of creatures. No angel of the nearer presence, no prophet sent (by God) has apprehended that. Profound study and reflection about that is a means to being abandoned (by God), a ladder to misfortune, and a step towards rebellion (against God). The truly cautious man (avoids this) by thought or reflection or suggestion. God has concealed the knowledge of predestination from His creatures and excluded them from His intention as He said: 'He is not questioned about what He does, but they are questioned' (11.23). Whoever asks why He did (something) has rejected the judgement of scripture and become one of the unbelievers.
15. This is the sum of what is required by the saints of God whose hearts are enlightened. This is the rank of those who are advanced in knowledge. For knowledge is twofold: existent knowledge about the creation and lost (or non-existent) knowledge about the creation. To reject the existent knowledge and to claim to have the non-existent is unbelief. Faith is only established where the existent knowledge is accepted and the search for the non-existent abandoned.
16. We believe in the Table and the Pen and all that (the Pen) wrote upon (the Table). If all creatures agreed about a thing of which God had written (on the Table) that it exists, (and purposed) to make it non-existent, they would not be able for that; and if all creatures agreed about a thing which God had not written on (the Table as existing), (and purposed) to make it existent, they would not be able for that. The Pen has become dry by (writing) what exists until the day of resurrection.
17. What missed a person could not have hit him, and what hit a person could not have missed him. People ought to know that God had previous knowledge of every existent in His creation, and by His will predetermined that (existent) carefully and finally, (in such a way) that in (His creation) in heaven and earth there is no contradiction, no repetition, no mistake, no change, no alteration, no deficiency and no excess. That belongs to faith and to the

principles of knowledge and to the acknowledgement of the oneness and Lordship of God; as God has said in His glorious book: 'and He created everything and predetermined it' (25.2); and also: 'And the affair of God was a predetermination predetermined' (33.38). Woe to whoever becomes opposed to God about predestination, and brings an unsound heart to reflect upon it! By his wrong idea of searching out the unseen he has sought a secret concealed, and by what he said about it has become a wicked liar

18. The Throne and the Sedile are a reality, as God made clear in His glorious book. He is independent of the Throne and what is below it; He comprehends everything above it, and has made His creation unable to comprehend (that).
19. We say that God took Abraham as a friend[3] and addressed Moses directly.
20. We believe in the angels and the prophets and the books sent down to the messengers; and we bear witness that they followed the clear truth. We call those who have our Qibla Muslims (and) believers, so long as they continue to acknowledge what the Prophet brought, and to count true all he said or reported.
21. We do not engage in discussion about God and we do not argue violently about (our) religion. We do not dispute about the Qur'ān, but we know that it is the Speech of the Lord of the Worlds; with it the Faithful Spirit[4] came down and taught it to the prince of the first and the last, Muḥammad. It is the speech of God, and no speech of the creatures equals it. We do not say it is created, and we do not oppose the community of the Muslims.
22. We do not consider as an unbeliever any of the people of the Qibla by reason of a sin, so long as he does not consider it lawful. We do not say: Where there is faith a sin does not harm the doer. We hope for Paradise for the believers who do good, but we are not certain of it, and do not bear witness to them (as having attained it). We seek forgiveness for their evil deeds and we fear for them, but we do not despair of them. Certainty (of Paradise) and despair both turn people away from the religion, and the way of truth for the people of the Qibla lies between them. A person does not depart from faith except by the denial of what caused him to enter it.
23. Faith is confessing with the tongue and counting true with the heart that all that God has sent down in the Qur'ān and all that is correctly (reported) from the Messenger of God, (both) of revealed truth and of explanation – that all that is a reality. Faith is one and its people in principle are equal; but one is superior to another truly in piety, in opposition to desire and in adherence to what is worthier. The believers, all of them, are friends (saints) of the

Merciful; the noblest of them in God's sight is the one who is most obedient and who follows the Qur'ān most closely.[5]

24. Faith is faith in God, His angels, His books, His messengers, the Last Day and God's predetermination of the good and the bad, of the sweet and the bitter. We believe in all that. We do not distinguish between His messengers but count all of them true in respect of (the revelations) they brought.
25. Those who commit great sins are in Hell, but not everlastingly if, when they died, they were monotheists, even though after they met God they did not repent and acknowledge (their sins). They are in (the sphere of) God's will and judgement; if He wills, He pardons and forgives them out of His grace; as God has said: 'God does not forgive being given a partner (sc. polytheism), but forgives what is less than that to whom He wills' (4.48, 116). If He wills, out of His justice He punishes them in hell to the measure of their offence; then in His mercy, and at the intercession of the intercessors among the people obeying Him, He removes them from Hell and raises them to His Paradise. That is because God is the guardian of those who acknowledge Him and does not set them in (? the lower of) the two mansions, like the people denying Him who are destitute of His guidance and have not received His protection. O God, Protector of Islam and its people, cause us to hold firmly to Islam until we meet Thee so (sc. as Muslims).
26. We approve of formal worship behind any of the people of the Qibla, (whether) upright or sinful, and on behalf of those of them who have died. We do not assign any of them to Paradise or Hell, and we do not bear witness against them of unbelief or idolatry or hypocrisy, so long as nothing of that is clearly evident in them, but we leave their secret hearts to God.
27. We do not approve of the sword against any of the community of Muḥammad, except him against whom the sword is obligatory. We do not approve of going out in (rebellion) against our imāms and the administrators of our affairs, even although they act wrongfully towards us, and we do not summon (others to rebel) against them and do not withdraw a hand from obeying them. We consider that obedience to them in (their) judging and administering of affairs belongs to obedience to God as something prescribed by God; and we pray for soundness and pardon for them.
28. We follow the Sunna and the Community, and we avoid unorthodoxy, disagreement and sectarianism. We love the people of justice and fidelity, and we loathe the people of wrongdoing and treachery. We say, where we have no certain knowledge of something, that God knows best.

29. We approve the moistening of the sandals both in journeying and at home, as is found in reports.
30. The Pilgrimage and the Jihād are two duties which are to be performed along with those of the imāms of the Muslims in authority, whether upright or sinners, (and they continue duties) until the day of resurrection; the evil of an evildoer does not cancel them, and the justice of a just person does not diminish them.
31. We believe in the noble scribes, and that God has made them watchers over us; we believe in the angel of death who is entrusted with (the task of) seizing the souls of (people in) the worlds.
32. We believe in the punishment of the tomb, and in delight there for whoever is worthy of it. We believe in the interrogation by Munkar and Nakīr of the dead person in his tomb about his Lord, his religion and his prophet; (this is) as related in the reports from the Messenger of God and his Companions. The tomb is one of the gardens of Paradise or one of the pits of Hell.
33. We believe in the resurrection after death and in the recompensing of (a person's) works on the day of resurrection, in the scrutiny and the reckoning, in the reading of the book (recording deeds), in reward and punishment, in the Bridge and the Balance. Paradise and Hell are (already) created, and will never disappear or cease to exist. God created Paradise and Hell before the creation (of the world), and (then) created for each of them a people; some He willed for Paradise out of His grace, and some He willed for Hell out of His justice.
34. Everyone does what he was made ready for, and moves towards what he was created for. Good and evil are determined for human beings. The acting-power through which the act takes place, such as the succour (from God) which the creature may not be characterised as possessing, comes to be along with the act. On the other hand, the acting-power, insofar as it depends on soundness (of body), capability, strength, and absence of defect in instruments, exists before the act. With this (meaning) is connected the discussion (of such matters), since, as God has said: 'God does not impose (duties) on a soul beyond its capability' (2.286). Human acts are the creation of God and the acquisition of the human beings. God imposes on them (as duties) only what they can compass, and they compass only what He imposes on them. That is the interpretation of the saying, 'There is no might and no power save with God, the High, the Mighty'. It means that no-one makes any scheme or movement or shift to disobey God without God's assistance, and that no-one acts obediently and perseveres in that without God's succour.

35. Everything comes about by the will, knowledge, decree and predetermination of God. His will is stronger than all wills, His volition than all volitions. His decree is stronger than all devices. Only what He wills comes about. God does what He wills, and He is never a wrongdoer. He is too holy to experience evil or trial, free from all shame and ugliness. 'He is not questioned about what He does, but they are questioned' (21.23).
36. In the prayer and alms of the living, there is a benefit for the dead. God answers prayers and satisfies needs. He rules everything, but nothing rules over Him. Nothing is independent of Him for the twinkling of an eye; whoever fancies he can be independent of Him for the twinkling of an eye is an unbeliever, one of the people of perdition.
37. God is angered and pleased, not as one of His creatures.
38. We love the Companions of the Messenger of God. We do not love any one of them specially, and we do not dissociate ourselves from any of them. We hate him who hates them and speaks other than good of them; we speak only good of them. Loving them is religion and faith and well-doing; hatred of them is unbelief and hypocrisy and presumption.
39. The caliphate, after the Messenger of God, was settled first on Abū Bakr al-Ṣiddīq, giving him precedence and setting him above all the community; then on ʿUmar ibn al-Khaṭṭāb; then on ʿUthmān ibn ʿAffān; then on ʿAlī ibn Abī Ṭālib. These are the rightly-guided caliphs, the well-directed imāms.
40. We love the ten whom the Messenger of God named and assured of paradise. We bear witness that they are in Paradise, according to the witness of the Messenger of God and his word which is truth. They are: Abū Bakr, ʿUmar, ʿUthmān, ʿAlī, Ṭalḥa, al-Zubayr, Saʿd, Saʿīd, ʿAbd al-Raḥmān ibn ʿAwf, Abū, ʿUbayda ibn al-Jarrāḥ. They are the trusty ones of this community.[6]
41. Whoever speaks well of the Companions of the Messenger of God, of his wives pure from stain, and of his descendants, free from all filth, is clear of hypocrisy. The ancient doctors of earlier and later generations and those who came after them, who (studied) ḥadīths and reports and who (studied) law and reflective thought, are not spoken of except for what is noble; whoever speaks evil of them is not on the (true) way.
42. We do not set any one of the saints above any of the prophets, but we say, 'One prophet is more excellent than all the saints'; we believe in (the saints') wonder-miracles that have come to our knowledge and have been soundly reported by trustworthy persons.

43. We believe in the signs of the Hour, (such as) the coming forth of the Dajjāl, the descent from heaven of ʿĪsā ibn Maryam, the rising of the sun in the west, and the coming forth of the Beast of the earth from his lair.
44. We do not give credence to diviners or sorcerers, or to anyone who makes claims contrary to the Book, the Sunna and the consensus of the community.
45. We consider (the main body of) the community as true and correct, and the sect as deviation and punishment. The religion of God in heaven and earth is one, namely, Islam. (God) said: 'Religion in God's sight is Islam' (3.19); and also: 'he who desires a religion other than Islam, it will not be accepted from him, and in the world to come he will be among the losers;' (3.85); and also: 'I have chosen Islam as a religion for you' (5.3). It lies between excess and deficiency, between anthropomorphism and denial (of God's attributes), between absolute determinism and (human) power, between assurance and despair.

This is our religion and our creed, openly and secretly, and we are clear towards God from everyone who opposes what we have said in our exposition. We ask God to establish us in it, to seal our possession of it, and to guard us from differing fancies, deviant opinions and corrupt doctrines, such as (those of) the Mushabbiha, the Jahmiyya, the Jabriyya, the Qadariyya and others who oppose the community and league themselves with the erring. From these we are clear, and in our eyes they are erring and perishing. And with God is protection.

NOTES

1 Purity of conception has been adopted as a translation of *tanzīh*. It means acceptance of God's attributes while avoiding anthropomorphism.

2 The pledge refers to a Qur'ānic verse (7.172). God brought the whole progeny of Adam before Him and made them acknowledge that He was their Lord, so that they could not plead ignorance on the Day of Judgement.

3 The Qur'ān (4.125) says that God took Abraham as a friend (*Khalīl*). Though Christians are mostly unaware of the fact, Abraham is spoken of as God's friend in the Bible: 2 Chronicles 20.7; Isaiah 41.8; James 2.23.

4 The Faithful Spirit is Gabriel; but this was only one of several 'manners' (*kayfiyyāt*) of revelation.

5 This article expresses the Ḥanafite view which excludes works. It is unusual to speak of all believers as 'friends' (*awliyā'*) of God, since *awliyā'* is usually restricted to 'saints' as in §42.

6 The names are in fuller form in the shorter Ḥanbalite creed, §14.

The Testament of Abū Ḥanīfa

The *Testament* (*waṣiyya*) ascribed to Abū Ḥanīfa is an anonymous work from his school, and is probably not earlier than 850 in view of various discussions to which it refers. The text used is found along with a commentary published in Hyderabad in 1321/1903. There is a translation in A. J. Wensinck's *Muslim Creed*, pp. 124–31, and his numbering of articles has been retained.

1. Faith is professing with the tongue, counting true with the mind and knowing with the heart. Professing alone is not faith, because, if that was faith then all the hypocrites would be believers. Similarly, knowledge alone is not faith, because, if that was faith, then all the people of the Book would be believers.[1] God said about the hypocrites: 'God bears witness that the hypocrites are lying' (68.1); and God said about the People of the Book: 'Those to whom We have given the Book know it as they know their sons' (2.146; 6.20).
2. Faith neither increases nor decreases. Its decrease can only be conceived by an increase of unbelief, and its increase can only be conceived by a decrease of unbelief; and how is it possible that one person at one time should be (both) a believer and an unbeliever?
3. The believer is truly a believer, and the unbeliever is truly an unbeliever. There is no doubt about (a person's) faith, just as there is no doubt about (a person's) unbelief, because of (God's) word: 'These are truly believers, and these are truly unbelievers' (4.150).[2]
4. Those of the community of Muḥammad who sin are all believers and not unbelievers.
5. Works (action) are other than faith, and faith is other than works. The proof of this is that at many times the believer is exempted from works, but it is not possible to say that he is exempted from faith. Thus God exempts women menstruating or in labour from formal worship, but it is not possible to say that He has exempted them from faith and has ordered them to give up faith. The lawgiver has said to (such a woman), 'Give up fasting and fulfil it later', but it is not possible to say, 'Give up faith and later fulfil it'. It is possible too to say, 'Almsgiving is not incumbent on the poor man', but it is not possible to say, 'Faith is not incumbent on the poor man'.

6. We assert that the predetermination (both) of the good and of the bad is entirely from God. If someone supposes that the predetermination of good and bad is from other than God, he would be an unbeliever in God, and his assertion that (God) is one would be invalid.
7. We assert that works are of three (kinds): obligatory, supererogatory and sinful. Obligatory (works) are in accordance with God's command, His will, His love, His good pleasure, His decree, His predetermination, His creation, His judgement, His knowledge, His succour and His writing on the Preserved Table. Sinful (works) are in accordance not with God's command but with His will, not with His love but with His decree, not with His good pleasure but with His predetermination and His creation, not with His succour but with His abandonment and His knowledge, not with His approval (?)[3] but with His writing on the Preserved Table.
8. We assert that God has seated Himself on the Throne without there being any necessity for Him (to do so), and without His being settled on it. He keeps the Throne and what is other than the Throne without any need (for Him to do this). If He had such a need, He would not have had power for bringing the world into existence and for ordering it, just as the created beings (have no such power). If He had a need to sit and to be settled (on the Throne), where was God before the creation of the Throne? May God be elevated far above (all that).
9. We assert that the Qur'ān is the Speech of God, uncreated, and His revelation and His sending down. It is not He and not other than He, but is His attribute in reality. It is written in the copies, recited by the tongues, remembered in the breasts, but not inhering in them. The ink, paper and writing are created, because they are the works of human beings; but the speech of God is uncreated, because the writing, the letters, the words and the signs (or verses) are an indication of the Qur'ān (on account of) the human beings' need for them. The Speech of God subsists in His essence, and its meaning is understood by these things. He who says that the Speech of God is created is an unbeliever in God the Mighty. God is worshipped, but does not cease to be as He was; and His speech is recited, written and remembered without being separated from Him.[4]
10. We assert that the most excellent of this community after our prophet Muḥammad is Abū Bakr al-Ṣiddīq, then 'Umar, then 'Uthmān, then 'Alī. (This is because of God's word): 'Those who go before, those who go before, these are the ones brought near in

gardens of delight' (56.10–12). Each one who goes before (or is earlier as caliph) is more excellent, and every pious believer loves them, and every base hypocrite hates them.

11. We assert that the human being with his acts, his profession (of belief) and his knowledge is created. Since the one acting is created, it is all the more (true) that his acts are created.
12. We assert that God created the creatures and that they had no ability, because they were weak and impotent, and God is their creator and sustainer; as He said: 'God created you, then sustained you, then causes you to die, ten makes you alive (again)' (30.40).
13. Financial gain is lawful and the acquiring of wealth is lawful, but the acquiring of wealth from what is unlawful is unlawful.
14. People are in three classes: the believer sincere in his faith; the unbeliever upholding his unbelief; and the hypocrite dissembling his hypocrisy. God has prescribed works for the believer, faith for the unbeliever, and sincerity for the hypocrite; as He said: 'O people, fear your Lord' (4.1; 22.1; 32.33); that is to say, 'O believers, obey; O unbelievers, have faith; and O hypocrites, be sincere'.
15. We assert that acting-power comes to be along with the act, not before the act and not after the act. If it existed before the act, then the person would be independent of God at the time of his need (to act), and this is contrary to the assertion of scripture, where (God) says: 'He is the rich and you are the poor' (47.38). If it was after the act, that would be impossible, for it would be the occurrence of an act without acting-power. The creature has no ability for an act, except when the acting-power (received) from God accompanies (the act).
16. We assert that the moistening of the sandals is obligatory for one remaining (at home) for a night and a day and for one travelling for three days and nights. (This is) because a ḥadīth in this sense has been recorded. He who denies this is in danger of unbelief, since it (is based on what) is near to being a widely-transmitted report. The shortening (of the formal-worship) and the breaking of the fast are allowable for those travelling by a text of scripture; as (God) said: 'When you go about on the land, no fault rests on you if you shorten the formal worship' (4.101); and as He said in respect of fasting: 'He of you who is sick or on a journey, (let him fast the same) number of other days' (2.184f.).
17. We assert that God ordered the Pen to write. The Pen said, 'What shall I write, O Lord?' God said, 'Write what is happening until the day of resurrection'; as He said: 'Everything they did is in the books, and every small and great (sin) is written down' (54.52f.).[5]
18. We assert that the punishment of the tomb undoubtedly exists.

19. We assert that the interrogation by Munkar and Nakīr is a reality, because of ḥadīths which have been transmitted.
20. Paradise and Hell are a reality, and they are now (already) created. They will not become non-existent nor will the people in them; as (God) said in respect of the believers: '(Paradise) is prepared for the pious' (3.133); and in respect of the unbelievers: '(Hell) is prepared for the unbelievers' (2.24; 3.131). He created them for reward and punishment.
21. We assert that the Balance is a reality; as (God) said: 'We appoint just balances for the day of resurrection' (21.47).
22. We assert that the reading of the book (recording one's deeds) on the day of resurrection is a reality; as (God) said: 'Read your book; you yourself are sufficient today (to state) the account against you' (17.14).
23. We assert that God will bring these souls (back) to life after death and will raise them up on a day whose length is 50,000 years, for requital, reward and the paying of dues; as (God) says: 'God will raise up those in the tombs' (22.7).
24. We assert that the meeting of God with the People of Paradise is a reality, (but it is to be understood) amodally, not in anthropomorphic (terms), and not as being in a (particular) direction.
25. The intercession of our prophet Muḥammad is a reality for all the People of Paradise, even for him who had committed a great sin.
26. We assert that after the great Khadīja, 'Ā'isha is the most excellent of the women of the world. She is the mother of the believers, kept pure from adultery and free from what the Rawāfiḍ say (accusing her). Whoever bears witness against her of adultery is himself the child of adultery.
27. We assert that the People of Paradise are in Paradise everlastingly and the People of Hell in Hell everlastingly; as (God) said in respect of the believers: 'These are the People of Paradise and are in it everlastingly'; and in respect of the unbelievers: 'These are the People of Hell and are in it everlastingly' (2.82, 81; etc.).

NOTES

1 The Qur'ānic reference to the People of the Book is obscure, but seems to mean that they have no difficulty in recognising revelation as revelation.

2 There is here a rejection of the practice of *istithnā'*, 'expression of uncertainty', accepted by the Ḥanbalites.

3 'Approval' renders *ma'rifa*, where the text is probably corrupt.

4 This creed has no mention of the 'utterance' (*lafẓ*) of the Qur'ān, but speaks of what people hear as an 'indication' (*dalāla*) of it. In the later ninth century, other thinkers held somewhat similar views; cf. *Formative Period*, p. 284.

5 The article seems to speak of books in which God's predetermination of all acts is written, whereas the Qur'ānic verses speak rather of books written as records of what has been done; cf. §22 and Al-Qayrawānī, §28.

A Later Ḥanafite Creed

This is the creed called by Wensinck *Al-Fiḳh al-Akbar II.* There is a text (with commentary) in the Hyderabad volume which contains the *Testament,* and this has been used here. This creed also is by an anonymous Ḥanafite author. Wensinck's suggestion (*Muslim Creed,* p. 240) that it might be by al-Ash'arī is impossible, because he failed to appreciate the difference in the definition of faith between the Ḥanafites and the Ḥanbalites (and al-Ash'arī). The discussion of the attributes of God suggests that this creed is somewhat later than the *Testament.*

1. The root of the assertion of (God's) unity and of sound belief is that one must say: 'I believe in God, His angels, His books, His messengers, the resurrection after death, the predetermination by God of both good and evil, the reckoning (of human deeds on the Last Day), the Balance, and Paradise and Hell; and that all these are real.'
2. (a) God is one, not in the sense of number, but in the sense of having no partner. He has not begotten (a child), nor was He Himself begotten. There is no-one like Him; He does not resemble anything of His creation nor does anything of His creation resemble Him. He always has been and always will be, with all His names and attributes, both those belonging to His essence and those belonging to His activity.

   (b) Those belonging to His essence are: life, power, knowledge, speech, hearing, seeing and will; those belonging to His activity are: creating, making provision for (sustaining), producing, initiating, making and other attributes of action.

   (c) He always has been and always will be with His attributes and His names. No attribute or name is originated. He has from eternity been knowing by His knowledge, and His knowledge is an attribute from eternity; (He has also been) powerful by His power, and his power is an attribute from eternity; likewise speaking by His speech, and His speech is an attribute from eternity; also creating by His creativity, and His creativity is an attribute from eternity; also acting by His (power of) action and His (power of) action is an attribute from eternity.

   (d) The one acting is God, and the (power of) action is His attribute from eternity; the result of action is created, but the action of God is uncreated. His attributes are from eternity, not originated and not created. Whoever says they are created or originated, or who is uncertain (suspends judgement) or doubts these two (points), is an unbeliever in God.

3. (a) The Qur'ān is the Speech of God, written in the copies, remembered (preserved) in the hearts, recited by the tongues, and sent down (from God) to the Prophet. Our utterance of the Qur'ān is created, our writing of it is created, our reciting of it is created, but the Qur'ān is uncreated.

   (b) What God mentions in the Qur'ān (as a report about) Moses and the other prophets, and (about) Pharaoh and Satan, is all the speech of God reporting about them. The speech of God is uncreated, but the speech of Moses and of the others of the creatures is created; the Qur'ān as the speech of God is from eternity, but not their speech. Moses heard the speech of God, as in the verse, 'God spoke with Moses' (4.162). God was speaking before He spoke to Moses, just as He was creating from eternity before He created creation. When He spoke to Moses, He spoke to him with His speech which is His attribute from eternity.

   (c) All His attributes are different from the attributes of created beings. He knows, but not as our knowledge is; He is powerful, but not as our power is; He sees, but not as our sight is; He speaks not as our speech is; and He hears not as our hearing is. We speak by means of organs and letters, but God speaks without organs and letters. Letters are created, but the speech of God is uncreated.

4. God is a thing, not as the (other) things. The meaning of 'thing' is what is established. (God is) without body, without substance[1] and without accident. He has no limit, no opposite, no rival, none similar to Him. He has a hand, a face and a self (or soul),[1] as he mentioned in the Qur'ān. When God mentions in the Qur'ān His face, His hand and His self, these are His attributes amodally. It is not said that His hand is His power or His grace, because that would abolish the attribute; such is the view of the Qadariyya and the Mu'tazila. On the contrary, His hand is His attribute amodally, and His anger and His good pleasure are two amodal attributes.

5. God has created the things not from any (pre-existent) thing. God was from eternity knowing about the things before their existence. He it was who predetermined the things and decreed them. Nothing exists in this world or the world to come except by His will, His knowledge, His decree, His predetermination and His writing of it on the Preserved Table; but His writing of it is descriptive and not decisive. His decree, His predetermination and

His will are His attributes from eternity amodally. God knows the (currently) non-existent in its state of non-existence as non-existent; and He knows how it will be when He causes it to be. He knows the existent in its state of existence as existent, and He knows the manner of its coming to exist. God knows (the person) standing in the state of his standing as standing, and, when he sits, He knows him as sitting, although there is no change in His knowledge and nothing new in His knowledge; but the change and the difference are originated in the created beings.

6. (a) God created the created beings free from unbelief and belief. Then He addressed them, giving them orders and prohibitions. Then certain of them disbelieved; their denial and rejection of the truth was by God's abandoning them. Certain of them believed, (showing this) by their action, their affirmation and their counting true; and (this was) by God's succour and His help.

   (b) God took the posterity of Adam[2] from his loins and endowed them with intellect. Then He addressed them, commanding them to believe and to abstain from unbelief. They then acknowledged His lordship, and this was faith (belief) on their part. In this religious state, people are born. Whoever afterwards became an unbeliever deviated from this and changed, while whoever afterwards believed and counted true remained and continued in it.

   (c) God did not compel any of His creatures to be unbelievers or believers. He did not create them either as believers or as unbelievers, but as individuals, and faith and unbelief are the acts of human beings. The person who turns to faith (from unbelief) God knows as an unbeliever in the state of his unbelief; and if he afterwards turns to faith, God knows him as a believer in his state of faith, and God loves him; but there is no change in God's knowledge or His attribute.

   (d) All the acts of human beings – their movements as well as their resting – are truly their own acquisition; but God creates them and they all come about by His will, knowledge, predetermination and decree.

7. All acts of obedience are obligatory because of God's command, desire, approval, knowledge, will , decree and predetermination. All acts of disobedience come about through His knowledge, decree, predetermination and will, but not according to His desire, approval or command.
8. All the prophets are immune from sins, both small and great, and from unbelief and shameful deeds, but they may stumble or make mistakes.
9. Muḥammad is God's beloved, His servant, His messenger, His

prophet, His chosen and elect. He did not serve idols, nor was he at any time an idolater, even for a moment. He never committed any sin, small or great.

10. The most excellent of persons after the Messenger of God is Abū Bakr al-Ṣiddīq, then ʿUmar ibn-al-Khaṭṭāb al-Fārūq, then ʿUthmān ibn-ʿAffān (he of the two lights), then ʿAlī al-Murtaḍā. We adhere to all of these. We name all the Companions of the Messenger of God only by way of praise.
11. We declare no Muslim an unbeliever on account of sin, even a great one, provided he does not declare it lawful. We do not exclude him from (the sphere of) faith, but say he is truly a believer; he maybe a believer of bad conduct, but he is not an unbeliever.
12. The moistening of the sandals is commendable. The additional acts of formal worship (during Ramaḍān) are commendable.
13. Formal worship is valid behind any believer, whether he is upright or sinful.
14. We do not say that sins will do no harm to the believer, nor do we say that he will not enter Hell, nor do we say that, though he was sinful, he will remain there eternally, provided he left this world as a believer. We do not say, as do the Murji'ites, that our good deeds are accepted and our sins forgiven. We do say, however, that, when a person performs a good deed, fulfilling all its conditions so that it is free from any blame which might impair it, and not (subsequently) nullifying it by unbelief, apostasy or bad morals, but dying a believer, then God will not overlook it, but will accept it from him and reward him for it. As for evil deeds, apart from idolatry or unbelief, if he who commits them dies as a believer but without repenting, he will be dependent on God's will; if He wills He punishes him in Hell, and if He wills He forgives him without punishing him in any way in Hell.
15. If any act is mixed with ostentation,[3] its reward is thereby forfeited, and similarly if it is mixed with vainglory.
16. The signs of the prophets and the wonder-miracles of the saints are real. As for those (unusual acts) performed by God's enemies, such as Satan, Pharaoh and the Dajjāl, which according to reports have taken place or will take place, we do not call them signs or wonder-miracles, but only the fulfilment of their wants. God fulfils the wants of His enemies, deluding them in this world and punishing them in the world to come; and thus they are betrayed and increase in error and unbelief. All these (acts) are actually-possible and possible.
17. God will be seen in the world to come. The believers will see Him

in Paradise with their bodily eyes, not anthropomorphically but amodally. There will be no distance between Him and His creatures.

18. Faith consists in professing (publicly) and counting true (in the mind). The faith of the people of Paradise and of earth does not increase or decrease. The believers are equal in faith and in the assertion of God's unity but they differ in respect of works, some being higher (than others).

Islam is submission to and compliance with the commands of God. Language distinguishes faith and Islam, but there is no faith without Islam, and Islam is not found without faith. The two are as back and belly (outward and inner). 'Religion' (*dīn*) is a term covering faith, Islam and all the commandments of the law.

19. We have a true knowledge of God as He describes Himself in His book, with all His attributes. Nobody, however, can truly serve God as is fitting for Him. A person serves Him (as best he can) according to the commands He has given in His book and in the Sunna of His messenger.

All the believers are equal in knowledge, subjective certainty, trust, love, inner quiet, fear, hope and faith; they differ in what is beyond faith.[4]

God acts generously towards human beings and also acts justly. Out of generosity He gives a reward double of what is deserved; in justice He punishes for sin. Out of grace He forgives.

20. The intercession of the prophets is real. The intercession of (our) Prophet on behalf of believers who have committed sins, even great sins and deserved punishment, is certainly real.

21. The weighing of (a person's) works (or acts) in the Balance on the day of resurrection is real.

The Basin of the Prophet is real.

The settling of accounts between adversaries on the day of resurrection is real. If they have no good works, the wrongs they have suffered from others are considered; and this is real.

Paradise and Hell are created and already exist; they will never cease to exist. The black-eyed (houris) will never die.

Punishment and reward by God are unceasing.

22. Out of grace God guides whoever He wills, and out of justice He leads astray whoever He wills. His leading astray means His abandoning (of a person); and that amounts to His not guiding that person towards deeds pleasing to Himself. This is justice on His part, as is His punishment of those abandoned on account of (?previous) sin. We may not say that Satan deprives the believer of his faith; but we say that a person gives up his faith and then Satan deprives him of it.

23. The interrogation of the dead in the tomb by Munkar and Nakīr is real. The reuniting of the body with the spirit in the tomb is real. The pressure and the punishment of the tomb is real, and will come about in the case of all the unbelievers, and may come about in the case of some sinful believers.
24. It is permissible to follow scholars in expressing the attributes of God in Persian, except in the case of God's hand. It is permissible to say *rūyi khudāy* (the face of God) not anthropomorphically but amodally.
25. God's being near or far is not to be understood in the sense of a shorter or longer distance, but in respect of (a person's) being honoured or not honoured. The obedient (person) is near God amodally and the disobedient (person) is far from Him amodally. Nearness, distance and coming closer apply to a person's intimate relation with God, as does God's being near in Paradise, and a person's standing before Him; all are to be understood amodally.
26. The Qur'ān was revealed to the Messenger of God, and is written in the copies. The verses of the Qur'ān, being the Speech of God, are all equal in excellence and greatness. Some, however, are superior (to others) for (purposes) of recitation or in respect of their contents. Such is the verse of the Throne (2.255), because it expresses God's majesty, greatness and (other) attributes; and thus it combines excellence for recitation with excellence of content. Other (verses) are excellent only for recitation such as those speaking of unbelievers, since those mentioned, the unbelievers, have no excellence. Similarly, all God's names and attributes are equal in greatness and excellence, without difference.
27. Qāsim, Ṭāhir and Ibrāhīm were sons of the Messenger of God. Fāṭima, Ruqayya, Zaynab and Umm Kulthūm were all daughters of the Messenger of God.
28. When a person is uncertain about any detail of the knowledge of God's unity, it is his duty for the time being to keep to what is sound in God's view. When he finds a scholar, he must consult him. He may not postpone the search (for a scholar). He is not excused for suspending judgement (in the matter), but becomes an unbeliever by his suspension of judgement.
29. The report of the ascension (of Muḥammad) is real, and whoever rejects it is an innovator and erring. The appearance of the Dajjāl, and of Yājūj and Mājūj, the rising of the sun from the west, the descent of 'Īsā from heaven and other signs of the Day of Resurrection, as described in sound ḥadīths, are real and will come about.

God guides whom He wills to the straight path.

NOTES

1 The translation here of *jawhar* as 'substance' has support from the commentary; but cf. 'Allāma-i-Ḥillī, 'God's negative attributes', §2. The Arabic *nafs* has been translated 'self', although 'soul' is also possible. It is not clear what precisely the author of the creed intended.

2 What is said about the posterity of Adam is a reference to the Qur'ānic verse 7.172, as in Al-Ṭaḥāwī, §12. The word *fiṭra* has been translated 'religious state'; there were discussions as to whether it meant Islam or a kind of natural religion; cf. Wensinck, *Muslim Creed*, p. 214f.

3 Wensinck's interpretation has been followed here, although *riyā'*, translated 'ostentation' can also mean 'hypocrisy'. Wensinck compares the New Testament injunction not to do one's good deeds so as to be seen of men.

4 What is 'beyond faith' is presumably works. Wensinck's translation seems to be mistaken.

Al-Qayrawānī

Ibn Abī Zayd al-Qayrawānī (c. 928–96) was a celebrated Mālikite jurist who lived mostly in Cairouan. This creed constitutes the first chapter of a treatise on Mālikite law known as the *Risāla*. It has been translated from the text in Ibn Abī Zayd al-Qayrawānī, *La Risāla*, edited and translated (into French) by Léon Bercher, Algiers, 1949. The position expressed in the creed is roughly that of the Ḥanbalites.

The necessary matters of religious (doctrine) which are to be uttered by the tongues and believed in the hearts.

1. There is to be faith (belief) in the heart and utterance by the tongue that God is one deity; there is no deity except Him; He has no like nor similar, no child nor parent, and no spouse nor partner. He is first without any beginning and last without any end.
2. The profundity of His attributes is beyond (human) characterisation; His affair is not comprehended by (human) reflection. (Human) reflection learns (something) from His signs, but it does not reflect on the nature of His essence, and does not comprehend anything of His knowledge except what He wills.
3. God's Throne[1] and Sedile extend over the heavens and the earth, and the keeping of these two is not difficult for Him.
4. God is the High, the Mighty, the Knowing, the Well-informed, the Disposer, the Powerful, the Hearing, the Seeing, the High, the Great.
5. God is above His glorious Throne by His essence, and He is in every place by His knowledge.
6. God created humankind; He knows what (evil suggestions) (a person's) soul whispers to him; He is nearer to him than his neck vein.
7. Not a leaf falls but God knows it; there is no seed in the darkness of the earth, and no plant green or withered, but it is in a clear book.
8. God is seated on the Throne; He has possession of (or preserves) the kingdom (? the material world).
9. To God belong the most beautiful names and the highest attributes; He is unceasingly (characterised) by all His attributes and His names. He is too sublime for His attributes to be created and His names originated.

10. God addressed Moses by His speech, which is an attribute of His essence, not one of His creatures. He appeared to the mountain[2] and it became levelled at His majesty.
11. The Qur'ān is the Speech of God; it is not a created thing so as to perish, nor the attribute of a created thing so as to cease.
12. (There must be) faith (belief) in (God's) predetermination, (both) the good and the bad of it, and the sweet and the bitter of it; all of that has been predetermined by God our Lord. The determinations (measures) of things are in His hand, and they have their source in His decree. He knows everything before its coming to be, and it proceeds according to His predetermination. There is no word nor act from human beings but He has decreed it and foreknown it. Does He not know those He has created, He who is the Gracious and the Well-informed?
13. In His justice, God leads astray whom He wills and abandons him, and by His grace He guides whom He wills and assists him. Thus (the way) is made easy by God's operation for each to (reach) the misery or happiness already (fixed for him) in God's foreknowledge and predetermination.
14. He is too sublime for there to be in His realm what He does not will, for there to be anyone independent of Him, or for there to be a creator of anything other than Himself. (He is) the Lord of human beings, the Lord of their works, the predeterminer of their movements and their appointed terms, and the sender of messengers to them for the establishing of a proof against them (sc. that they have known God's command and disobeyed).
15. Further, God sealed (or consummated) the office of messenger, warner and prophet with Muḥammad His prophet, making him the last of the messengers, a preacher (of good news), a warner and summoner to God by His permission, and a shining lamp. To him He sent down His wise book, through him He made plain His religion in its steadfastness, and by him He guided (people) in the straight path.
16. The Hour is undoubtedly coming, and God will raise up the dead; as He first created them, so will they return.
17. God has multiplied good things for His servants, the believers, on (their) repentance has forgiven their great evil-doings, and has pardoned their slight faults on their turning from the great sins; him who did not repent of the great sins He set on the way to what He wills.
18. God does not pardon the giving of partners to Himself (or idolatry), but He pardons what is less than that to whom He wills.
19. Him whom God has punished in Hell He takes out from it because

of his faith and brings into His Paradise; 'and whoever has done an atom's weight of good sees it' (99.7).

20. Through the intercession of the Prophet, God takes out from Hell him for whom (the prophet) intercedes of the great sinners of his community.
21. God has (already) created Paradise and has prepared it as an everlasting abode for His friends,[3] and has honoured them in it with the vision of His noble face. From Paradise He sent down Adam, His prophet and caliph (vicegerent), to His earth in accordance with what was already (fixed) in His foreknowledge. He has (already) created Hell and prepared it as an everlasting abode for him who has disbelieved in Him and deviated from His signs, His books and His messengers. Such (people) He has veiled from the vision of Himself.
22. God will come on the day of resurrection, with the angels in ranks, for the inspection of the peoples and the reckoning with them for reward and punishment. The Balances are placed to weigh the works of human beings; 'those whose balances are heavy are the successful' (23.102). (People) will be given the record of their works; 'He who is given his book in his right hand shall assuredly be reckoned with easily ... but he who is given his book behind his back ... those will roast in a blaze' (83. 7, 8, 10, 12).
23. The Bridge is a reality. Human beings pass over it according to the measure of their works. Those being saved move over it with great speed and escape the fire of Gehenna. A group are thrown to perdition in that by their works.
24. (There must be) belief in the Basin of the Messenger of God. To it his community come to drink, and he who has drunk of it will not thirst (again); but he who has changed and altered (his beliefs) will be repelled from it.
25. Faith is speech with the tongue, sincere devotion in the heart and works with the limbs. It increases with the increase of works, and decreases with their decrease, so that works bring about decrease or increase (of faith). The profession (speaking) of faith is perfected only by works, profession and works only by intention, and profession, works and intention only by conformity with the Sunna.
26. None of the people of the Qibla becomes an unbeliever through sin.
27. The martyrs are alive with their Lord, receiving sustenance. The spirits of the people of happiness (who will go to Paradise) remain in enjoyment until the day they are raised up, but the spirits of the people of misery (who will go to Hell) are being punished until the Day of Judgement. The believers are examined in their tombs and

interrogated; God confirms in the present life and in the world to come those who believe (in Him) with a firm speech.

28. Over human beings are guardians writing down their works. Nothing of these escapes the knowledge of their Lord. The angel of death takes away the spirits by the permission of his Lord.
29. The best of generations is the generation who saw the Messenger of God and believed in him. Next are those who followed them, and next are those who followed these. The most excellent of the Companions (of Muḥammad) are the rightly and truly guided caliphs, Abū Bakr, then ʿUmar, then ʿUthmān, then ʿAlī. Let not any of the Companions of the Messenger be mentioned except most honourably and without reference to what was disputed among them. They, above other people, deserve to have the best construction put upon (their conduct) and to have the best views attributed to them.
30. Obedience (is owed) to the imāms of the Muslims, both those who administer their affairs and their scholars. (It is a duty) to follow the sound ancient (authorities), to imitate the (examples) they left, and to ask pardon for them: and also to avoid disputation and argument in (matters of) religion, and to avoid all heretical innovations.

God's blessing on our master Muḥammad, His prophet, and on his family, his wives and his progeny; may He preserve them all.

NOTES

1 'Throne' (*ʿarsh*) has been inserted here. It is not in the printed text, but is required by the dual in the following clause; and it is used later in the creed.

2 For the mountain, see Al-Ashʿarī, §22 and note.

3 God's *awliyā'* or 'friends' here appear to be all the believers who enter Paradise, and not 'saints' in a restricted sense (which is a common meaning of the word).

Al-Ghazālī

There is a fairly full account of al-Ghazālī in the Introduction. The creed translated here (which was previously translated by D. B. Macdonald in his *Development*) is found in the second book of *The Revival of the Religious Sciences* (of which there is a complete translation by Nabih Amin Faris, *The Foundations of the Articles of Faith*, Ashraf, Lahore, 1963). There are many editions of *The Revival* (Iḥyā'). It is thought that this creed was intended for learning by heart by young Muslims, and it explains many points in greater detail than the others.

An exposition of the creed of the People of the Sunna (contained) in the two words of the Shahāda, which is one of the pillars of Islam.

Praise belongs to God ...

1. God is the witness who makes known to (His chosen people) that in His essence He is one, without partner, alone and without any like, enduring and without opposite, unique and without equal. He is one, pre-eternal with no first (state), from eternity without beginning, continuing in existence with no end (state), remaining to eternity without termination, stable and not cut short, lasting without being interrupted. He has not ceased, and will not cease, to be characterised by qualities[1] of majesty. He is unaffected by passing away and separation through the interruption of enduring (states) and the elapsing of appointed terms. Rather, He is the first and the last, the external and the internal, and He is knowing about everything.
2. God is not a body shaped nor a substance delimited and determinate. He does not resemble bodies either in being determinate or in being susceptible of division. He is not a substance, and substances do not inhere in Him; and He is not an accident, and accidents do not inhere in Him. He does not resemble any existing thing, and no existing thing resembles Him. Nothing is like Him, and He is not like anything. Measure does not limit Him, and boundaries do not contain Him.
3. God is seated on the Throne in the manner He stated, and with the meaning He willed for 'sitting'. He is not to be described as touching (it) or as being settled (on it) or being placed or inhering or moving away (from it). The Throne does not bear Him, but the

Throne and its bearers are borne by the grace of His power and subdued by His handgrasp. He is above the Throne and the heaven and everything to the bounds of the earth, and He is above in a way which does not bring Him nearer to the Throne and the heaven, as it does not take Him further from the earth and the ground. Rather, He is exalted by degrees from the Throne and the heaven, just as He is exalted by degrees from the earth and the ground. Despite that, He is near to every existent thing, and He is nearer to a human being than his neck vein (5.16). Over everything He is a witness, since His nearness does not resemble the nearness of bodies, just as His essence does not resemble the essence of bodies.

4. God does not inhere in anything, and nothing inheres in Him. He is exalted above being contained by space, and too holy to be bounded by time; on the contrary, He existed before He created time and space. He now has (the attributes) by which He was (previously characterised), and is distinguished from His creatures by His attributes. There is not in His essence what is other than He, nor in what is other than He is there (?anything of) His essence. He is exalted above change (of state) and movement. Originated things do not inhere (or subsist) in Him, and accidental (events) do not befall Him. Rather, He does not cease; through the qualities of His majesty He is beyond cessation, and through the attributes of His perfection He is independent of (or does not require) any further increase of perfection.
5. God in His essence is known by reason to exist. His essence is seen by the eyes in the enduring abode, as a favour from Him and a grace to the upright; and He completes His favour by (giving) sight of His noble countenance.
6. God is living, powerful, compelling, constraining. Shortcoming and impotence do not befall Him. Slumber and sleep do not take hold of Him. Passing away and death do not happen to Him. He is king of the worlds, the visible and the invisible, possessor of strength and might. He has authority and sovereignty. His it is to create and to command. The heavens are folded in His right hand, and created things are securely held in His grasp. He is alone in creating and producing; He is unique in bringing into existence and innovating. He created the creatures and their works, and determined their sustenance and their appointed terms. Nothing determined escapes His grasp. The changes of things are not outwith His power. The things that He has determined cannot be numbered, and the things that He knows are infinite.
7. God is knowing of all objects of knowledge, and comprehending of

all that happens from the bounds of earth to the highest heaven. He is knowing (in such a way) that not the weight of an atom in heaven or earth is outwith His knowledge. Indeed, He knows the creeping of the black ant on the hard rock in a dark night, He perceives the movement of the mote in the air, He knows what is secret and what is concealed, and is aware of the suggestions of the minds, the movements of the thoughts, and what is hidden in the hearts; and (He does this) by a knowledge pre-eternal and without beginning, with which He has not ceased to be characterised from the ages of ages, not by a knowledge which is originated, renewed and produced in His essence by inherence and change.

8. God is willing existent things and arranging originated things. In the visible and invisible worlds there is nothing little or much, small or great, good or bad, helpful or harmful, faith or unbelief, knowledge or ignorance, increase or decrease, obedience or disobedience, except by His decree and predetermination, His wisdom and His will. What He wills comes about, and what He does not will does not come about. Not the glance of an eye nor a sudden thought goes beyond His will. He is the one who begins (things) and restores, the one effecting what He wills. None opposes His command, and none repeats His decree. The human being cannot escape disobeying Him except by His succour and His mercy, and has no power to obey Him except by His will and His volition. If humankind, the jinn, the angels and the demons united to cause a single atom in the world to move, or to cause it to rest, apart from His volition and will, they would be unable for that. His will subsists in His essence beside all His attributes, and thus He has not ceased to be characterised as willing from all eternity the existence of things at the time He determined for them. They come into existence at their (proper) times as He willed from all eternity, neither too early nor too late. They occur in accordance with His knowledge and His will without change or alteration. He orders the affairs, but not (as human beings do) by arranging thoughts and awaiting a time, and so one matter does not keep Him from (doing) another.

9. God is hearing and seeing. He hears and sees, and nothing audible is beyond His hearing, even if it is hidden, and nothing visible is absent from His sight even if it is very small. Distance does not veil His hearing, and darkness does not repel His sight. He sees without eyeball or eyelid, and hears without earhole or ears, just as He knows without a heart, overwhelms without a limb and creates without an instrument. (This is) because His attributes do not resemble the attributes of created beings, just

as His essence does not resemble the essence of created beings.

10. God is speaking, (and in His speech) He commands, forbids, promises and threatens. He does this by speech which is pre-eternal and from eternity, subsisting in His essence. The speech of created beings does not resemble it. It is not a sound produced by the emission of air or the closing of the throat; and it is not letters made distinct by joining the lips or moving the tongue. The Qur'ān, the Torah, the Gospel and the Psalms are God's books sent down to His messengers. The Qur'ān is recited by the tongues, written in the copies, and remembered in the hearts; but despite this it is from eternity subsisting in God's essence, and it does not suffer division and separation by being transferred to the hearts and pages. Moses heard the speech of God without sound or letter, just as the upright see the essence of God in the world to come without substance or accident.
11. Since God has these attributes, He is living, knowing, powerful, willing, hearing, seeing, speaking; (and He is such) by having Life, Knowledge, Power, Will, Hearing, Sight and Speech, not by His mere essence (apart from these attributes).
12. There is no existent apart from God except what is originated by His act and proceeds from His justice; (and that) is the finest, most perfect, most complete and most just of manners. He is wise in His acts and just in His decrees. His justice is not analogous to the justice of human beings, since wrong doing is conceivable for the human being when he is dealing with the property of others; but wrongdoing from God is inconceivable, since He does not encounter property belonging to another, such that His dealing with it would be wrongdoing. What is apart from God – human beings, jinn, angels, demons, the heaven and the earth, animals, plants and inanimate objects, substance and accident, what is perceived and what is sensed – all this is originated. By His power, God brought it into being after its non-existence, and made it something after it had been nothing, since from eternity He alone was existent and there was nothing along with Him. After that, He originated creation as a manifestation of His power and a realisation of what He had previously willed, and of what from eternity had been truly His word. (He did this) not because of any lack of it or need for it.
13. God showed favour (to His creatures) by creating them, bringing them into being and imposing laws on them, though there was no necessity (to do this); and He showed generosity by doing good to them and helping them, though He was not obliged (to do so). His it is to favour, to benefit, to be gracious, to bestow gifts, since He

has power to inflict various kinds of punishment on human beings, and to try them with various forms of pain and illness. If He did that, it would be justice on His part, and it would not be something foul or wrong. He rewards His servants, the believers, for their acts of obedience; (and He does so) in accordance with His kindness and His promise, not on the basis of their rights (or deserts) or of an obligation to them. No act on behalf of anyone is obligatory for Him, and wrongdoing on His part is inconceivable, while no-one has any binding right against Him.

14. God's right to acts of obedience is an obligation for created beings, because He made it so by the tongues of His prophets and by pure reason. Moreover, in sending prophets He showed their truthfulness by clear evidentiary miracles; and they communicated His commands, prohibitions, promises and threats. It is obligatory for human beings to count true what they brought.
15. The second word (of the Shahāda) is to bear witness to the messengership of the messenger. God sent the illiterate[2] prophet of Quraysh, Muḥammad, with His message to the totality of Arabs and non-Arabs, of jinn and humankind. He abrogated by (Muḥammad's) law the laws (of previous prophets), except what He confirmed of them. He set (Muḥammad) above the other prophets, and made him prince of the human race. The faith (consisting) of witness to the unity (of God) in the phrase 'there is no deity except God' He declared to be incomplete where it was not accompanied by the witness to the Messenger in the phrase 'Muḥammad is the Messenger of God'.
16. God made it compulsory for created beings to count (Muḥammad) true in all that was reported from him about the affairs of this world and the world to come. (In particular), the faith of a human being is not acceptable until he believes in what (Muḥammad) reported about (conditions) after death.
17. The first of (such matters) is the interrogation by Munkar and Nakīr. These are two awe-inspiring and terrifying beings who make the human person sit up in his grave with both spirit and body and question him about his assertion of (God's) unity and the messengership (of Muḥammad). They say, 'Who was your Lord? What was your religion? Who was your prophet?' They are the two examiners in the grave, and their interrogation is the first test after death.
18. (The person of faith) should also believe in the punishment of the tomb, that it is a reality and that its judgement is just for body and spirit according to what God willed.
19. He should also believe in the Balance with its two pans and its

tongue. To characterise its size, it is like the (different) layers of the heavens and the earth. In it are weighed the works (of human beings) by the power of God. The weights (used) that day will have the weight of an atom or a mustard seed to ensure the precision of God's justice. The pages (recording) good deeds will be placed in a fine form in the pan of light, and the Balance will be weighed down by them according to the measure of their degrees in God's sight, (and this will happen) by His grace; the pages with evil deeds will be thrown in a foul form into the pan of darkness, and by God's justice they will have little weight in the Balance.

20. He should also believe that the Bridge is a reality. It is a bridge stretched over the back of Gehenna, sharper than a sword and finer than a hair. On it the feet of the unbelievers slip by God's judgement and bring them down to Hell, but the feet of the believers are kept steady on it by God's grace.
21. He should also believe in the Basin to which (people) go down, the Basin of Muḥammad. The believers drink from it before entering Paradise and after crossing the Bridge. Whoever takes a drink from it will never thirst again. Its breadth is a month's journey. Its water is whiter than milk and sweeter than honey. Round it are vessels whose number is as that of the stars in heaven. In it are two pipes which pour water into it from al-Kawthar.[3]
22. He should also believe in the Reckoning, and the differences of people in respect of it; one will be hard pressed in the reckoning, one will be treated leniently in it, and one will enter Paradise without a reckoning. (The latter) are those brought near. God will ask whom He wills of the prophets about the communicating of the message, and whom He wills of the unbelievers about their counting false of the messengers. He will ask the innovators about the Sunna, and the believers about (their) acts.
23. He should also believe that monotheists will be taken out of Hell after punishment. As a result, by the grace of God no monotheist will remain in Gehenna and no monotheist will be everlastingly in Hell.
24. He should also believe in the intercession of the prophets, then of the scholars, then of the martyrs, then of the other believers, each according to his dignity and his rank in the sight of God. He who remains of the believers without an intercessor will be taken out by God's grace. No believer will be everlastingly in Hell, but will be taken out from it provided there is an atom's weight of faith in his heart.
25. He should also hold the superiority of the Companions and their high rank, and also that the most excellent of the people after the

Prophet was Abū Bakr, then 'Umar, then 'Uthmān, then 'Alī. He should have a high opinion of all the Companions, and should praise them as God and his messengers praise (them).

All that is of what has been handed down in reports (ḥadīth) and witnessed to by transmitted statements. He who believes all that with certainty is of the People of Truth and the Company of the Sunna, and has kept clear of the band of error and the party of innovation. We ask God that we ourselves and all the believers may have perfect certainty and sure, sound steadfastness in religion, through His mercy who is the most Merciful. God bless our prince Muḥammad and every chosen servant (of God).

NOTES

1 The word 'qualities' is here used to translate *nu'ūt*. It was previously used by Wensinck to translate *ṣifāt*, which in this book is always 'attributes'. Whether there is any difference is not clear. The same word occurs in §4.

2 The Arabic *ummī* has here been translated 'illiterate' in accordance with the standard Muslim interpretation of the Qur'ānic word. Western scholars are fairly certain, however, that when the Qur'ān (7.157f.) called Muḥammad 'the *ummī* prophet' it originally meant 'the gentile (or non-Jewish) prophet'; cf. *Muhammad's Mecca*, 51–3.

3 Al-Kawthar is usually considered a river of Paradise; cf. Aḥmad ibn Ḥanbal, §12.

Al-Nasafī

Najm al-Dīn Abū Ḥafṣ al-Nasafī (1068–1142) belonged to the school of al-Māturīdī, and may have lived mostly in Samarqand. This short creed became very popular, and there were many commentaries and supercommentaries. The translation has been made from the text contained in *The Pillar of the Creed ...*, edited by W. Cureton, London, 1843, in conjunction with that contained in a Cairo edition of the commentary by al-Taftazānī (d. c. 1389), dated 1358/1939. Some slight differences between the two texts have been neglected. The creed was translated by D. B. Macdonald in his *Development*, pp. 308–15, and there is a translation of al-Taftazānī's commentary by E. E. Elder, *A Commentary on the Creed of Islam*, Columbia University Press, New York, 1950.

1. The People of Truth say that the real natures of things are established (or fixed), and that knowledge of them is really (knowledge). (This is) contrary to the view of the Sophists.[1]
2. The causes of knowledge for created beings are three: the sound senses, true report and reason. The senses are five: hearing, sight, smell, taste and touch; by each sense, information is given about (the class of objects) for which it is appointed. True report is of two kinds. One of these is the widely-transmitted report, that is, a report established by the tongues of (many) people, whose agreement on a falsehood is inconceivable. This is bound to give a necessary knowledge, such as the knowledge of former kings in past times and of distant lands. The second kind is the report of the messenger (who has been) attested by an evidentiary miracle (about what has come to him by revelation). This is bound to give deductive knowledge. The knowledge established by (such a report) resembles in certainty and fixity knowledge necessarily established (such as sense-knowledge and that from widely-transmitted reports). Reason, again, is also a cause of knowledge. What is established by immediate intuition is necessary, such as the knowledge that every thing is greater than its part. What is established by inference is acquired knowledge. Inspiration is not one of the causes of the knowing of the soundness (or truth) of a thing in the view of the People of Truth.
3. The world with all its parts is originated, since it (consists of)

substances (or individuals) and accidents. Substances are what is self-subsistent. A substance is either composite, that is, a body, or non-composite, such as the atom, which is the part which cannot be further divided. The accident is what is not self-subsistent but is originated in the bodies and atoms, such as colours, physical states,[2] tastes and smells.

4. The Originator of the world is God. He is the One, the Pre-eternal, the Living, the Powerful, the Knowing, the Wishing (or Willing), the Willing. He is neither accident nor body nor atom. He is neither formed nor limited nor multiple. He has neither portions nor parts, and He is not composite. He is not finite. He is not characterised by quiddity[3] nor by quality. He is not located in a place, nor does time pass over (or affect) Him. Nothing resembles Him. Nothing is outwith His knowledge and power.
5. God has pre-eternal attributes subsisting in His essence. They are not He and not other than He. They are: Knowledge, Power, Life, Strength, Hearing, Sight, Will, Volition, Activity, Creativity, Provision of sustenance (for creatures) and Speech.
6. God is speaking with a Speech which is a pre-eternal attribute for Him, and which is not of the class of letters and sounds. It is an attribute which excludes silence and defect. God speaks with this (attribute), commanding, prohibiting and making statements (or reporting).
7. The Qur'ān is the Speech of God, uncreated. It is written in the copies, remembered in the hearts, recited by the tongues, heard by the ears; but it does not inhere in these.
8. Causing-to-be is a pre-eternal attribute of God. It is His causing-to-be of the world and all its parts, not from eternity but at the time of its coming into existence in accordance with His knowledge and His will. (The attribute of causing to be) is other than what has been caused to be in our view.
9. Will is a pre-eternal attribute of God subsisting in His essence.
10. By reason, the vision of God (in Paradise) is possible; and by transmitted (reports) it is necessary that He should be seen. A proof based on oral (material) has been handed down showing that it is necessary that the believers should see God in the world to come. He is not seen in a place, nor in any direction from (the person) facing Him, nor by the coming together of light rays, nor with a fixed distance between the person seeing and God.
11. God is the creator of all the acts of human beings, whether (acts) of unbelief or faith, of obedience or disobedience. All these acts are by His will and volition, by His judgement, His decreeing and His determining. Human beings (perform) acts of choice for which

they are rewarded or punished. The good in them is with God's good pleasure, and the bad in them is not with His good pleasure.

12. The acting-power (in people) exists along with the act (not before it). It is the reality of the power by which the act comes to be. This name (acting-power) is used where the causes, instruments and limbs (involved in the act) are sound. (A person's) being genuinely liable (to obey the law) depends on this acting-power; a person is not liable for (carrying out) what is not within his capacity.
13. The pain existing in a (person) beaten as a result of human beating, and the broken (condition) of a glass after a human (act of) breaking, and similar things, are all created by God. The person has no function in the creating of these.
14. The one killed dies at his appointed term. The appointed term is one.
15. Unlawful (food) is (nevertheless) sustenance from God. Everyone receives in full his own sustenance, whether lawful or unlawful. It is inconceivable that a person should not eat his sustenance, or that his sustenance should be eaten by someone else.
16. God leads astray whom He wills, and guides whom He wills. It is not obligatory for God to do the best[4] for a human being.
17. The punishment in the tomb for unbelievers and for some sinful believers, and the bliss in the tomb[5] of the obedient people, are in accordance with God's knowledge and will. The interrogation by Munkar and Nakīr is established by proofs based on oral (reports). The raising of the dead is a reality. The Balance is a reality. The Book (recording a person's deeds) is a reality. The interrogation (by God) is a reality. The Basin is a reality. The Bridge is a reality. Paradise is a reality and Hell is a reality, and they are (already) created and existent. They are everlasting and will not pass away, and their people will not pass away.
18. A great sin does not exclude the believing person from faith and place him in unbelief (that is, does not make him an unbeliever). God does not forgive one who assigns partners to Him, but He forgives to whom He wills what is less than that of small and great sins. The punishing of a small sin is possible (for God) and also the forgiving of a great sin, provided this is not the considering lawful (of what is forbidden), for such considering lawful is unbelief.
19. The intercession of the messengers and of the élite is established for the case of those committing great sins. Those believers who commit great sins do not remain everlastingly in Hell.
20. Faith is the counting true of what (a messenger) has brought from God (as revelation) and the confessing of it. Works increase in themselves, but faith neither increases not decreases. Faith and

Islam are one (or the same). Where a person counts true and confesses, it is proper for him to say 'I am truly a believer', and he does not have to say 'I am a believer if God wills'.[6]

21. The happy one sometimes becomes miserable and the miserable one happy, but the change is in (the human experience) of happiness and misery, not in the making happy and the making miserable, for these are attributes of God, and there is no change in God or in His attributes.
22. In the sending of messengers (by God), there is wisdom. God has sent to humanity messengers who are human to bring good news, to warn and to make clear to people what they need (to know) about the affairs of the secular world and of religion. He confirmed (their genuineness) as messengers by evidentiary miracles, (that is, happenings) which are contrary to the natural order. The first of the prophets is Adam and the last of them is Muḥammad. A statement of their number has been handed down in some ḥadīths; but it is preferable that there should be no limit of number in naming (them). God has said (referring to previous messengers): 'Of some of them We have told you the stories, and of some We have not told you the stories' (40.78). When the number (of prophets and messengers) is stated, there is no security against some being included among them who are not of them, and some being excluded from them who are of them. All were reporting and conveying messages from God, and were truthful and sincere. The most excellent of the prophets is Muḥammad.
23. The angels are servants of God fulfilling His command. They are not characterised by masculinity or femininity.
24. God has books which He has sent down to His prophets. In them He has made clear His commands and His prohibitions, His promise and His threat.
25. The Ascension of the Messenger of God is a reality, (that is), when, while awake, he (was taken) bodily to heaven and then to what (place) on high God willed.
26. The wonder-miracles of the saints are a reality. The wonder-miracle appears for the saint as something contrary to the natural order, such as travelling a great distance in a short time, the appearance of food, drink and clothing when they are needed, walking on water or in the air, the speaking of inanimate objects and of animals, the warding-off of threatened injury, the guarding of an anxious person from his enemies, and other (similar) things. Such (an occurrence) is (at the same time) an evidentiary-miracle supporting the messenger, to one of whose community the wonder-miracle has occurred; for it shows that he is (truly) a saint,

since (a person) will not become a saint unless he counts true his religion, and his religion is the confession that his messenger is (indeed) a messenger.

27. The most excellent of humanity after our prophet is Abū Bakr al-Ṣiddīq, then 'Umar al-Fārūq, then 'Uthmān Dhu'l-nūrayn, then 'Alī al-Murtaḍā. The caliphate was in this order, and (lasted) thirty years. After that, the form of rule was kingly and princely.
28. The Muslims must have an imām (leader), who will see to the enforcing of their judgements, the carrying-out of their punishments, the defence of their frontiers, the equipping of their armies, the receiving of their alms, the controlling of violent men, thieves and highwaymen, the maintaining (of worship) on Fridays and festivals, the settling of the disputes which occur between people, the receiving of evidence regarding legal rights, the arranging of marriages for male and female minors who have no guardians, and the dividing of the spoils (of war). Further, the imām must be seen (publicly and recognised as imām), not hidden nor (merely) expected. He must be of the tribe of Quraysh and not of any other; but he is not restricted to the clan of Banū Hāshim or the descendants of 'Alī. It is not a condition (of his imāmate) that he be preserved from error, nor that he be the most excellent of the people of his time; but it is a condition that he should be of those who have full and complete authority, and an administrator with power to enforce the judgements, to preserve the frontiers of the sphere of Islam, and to ensure justice for the one wronged against the one wronging him. He is not to be removed from the imāmate because of transgressing (the divine law) or acting unjustly.
29. Formal worship is permitted behind any (leader), upright or sinful, and there may be formal worship on behalf of anyone, upright or sinful.
30. Only good should be spoken of the Companions (of Muḥammad).
31. We bear witness that Paradise is (promised) to the ten to whom the Prophet announced this.
32. We approve of the moistening of the sandals both when on a journey and when at home.
33. We do not prohibit wine made from dates.
34. The saint does not reach the level of the prophets. The (ordinary) person does not come to a position where (God's) commands and prohibitions and the scriptural texts in their external sense are no longer applicable to him. To turn from these to the interpretations of the people of internal meanings[7] is heresy. To reject the scriptural texts is unbelief. To regard sin as lawful is unbelief, to make light (of sin) is unbelief, and contempt for the law is unbelief.

35. To despair of God is unbelief, and to feel secure from God's (punishment) is unbelief. To count true what a diviner reports about the unseen is unbelief.
36. The non-existent[8] is not a thing.
37. In the prayer of the living for the dead, and in almsgiving for them, there is benefit for the dead. God answers prayers and supplies needs.
38. What the Prophet reported of the signs of the Hour, such as the appearance of the Dajjāl and of the beast of the earth and of Ya'jūj and Ma'jūj, and the coming-down of 'Īsā from heaven, and the rising of the sun in the west – all this is reality.
39. The interpreter (of texts) may sometimes be mistaken and sometimes be correct (in his interpretations).
40. The messengers of the human race are more excellent than the messengers of the angels, the messengers of the angels are more excellent than the generality of the human race, and the generality of the human race are more excellent than the generality of the angels.

NOTES

1 For the Sophists, see Wensinck, *Muslim Creed*, p. 251f.
2 The 'physical states' (*akwān*) are union, separation, movement, rest.
3 'Quiddity' represents the Arabic *mā'iyya* and 'quality' *kayfiyya*; for the latter, 'manner' is also possible. What precisely the author meant is not clear.
4 'What is best' is *al-aṣlaḥ*. For the discussions about this term, see EI² s.v.
5 The mention of 'bliss in the tomb' seems an innovation.
6 This is an implicit rejection of the Ḥanbalite view of *istithnā'*, expression of uncertainty.
7 The 'people of interior meaning' (*ahl al-bāṭin*) are usually called Bāṭiniyya; see EI², s.v.
8 The Arabic for 'non-existent' is *ma'dūm*.

Al-Ījī

ʿAḍud al-Dīn al-Ījī (c. 1281-1355) was a member of the Ashʿarite school of theology in Shiraz, where he seems to have spent the closing years of his life. The short creed here translated is commonly known as the ʿAḍudiyya, and commentaries on it have been written in many parts of the Islamic world. The translation is based on a manuscript in my possession and on an edition, published in Cairo in 1323/1905, of al-Dawānī's commentary together with two supercommentaries. Al-Ījī is also known for a lengthy theological work called *Al-Mawāqif*, which together with the commentary on it by al-Jurjānī fills four large volumes; more than half of this deals with the philosophical preliminaries, but nothing of these appears in the creed.

The Prophet said, 'My community will be divided into seventy-three sects, all of them in Hell except one'. He was asked who these (the saved) were. Those, he said, who believe as I myself and my Companions believe. The following are the articles of belief of the salvation-giving sect, who are the Ashʿarites; (they are what was agreed on by) the early (authoritative) ḥadīth-scholars and the Imāms of the Muslims and the People of the Sunna and the Community.[1]

1. The world is originated, and is capable of becoming non-existent.
2. Reflective thought with a view to (acquiring) knowledge of God is obligatory by revelation.[2] By reflective thought, knowledge is attained; and there is no need for a teacher.
3. The world has a Maker who has been from eternity. He has never ceased (to exist) and will never cease. His existence is necessary by His essence, and His non-existence is (known to be) impossible by reflective thought on His essence. There is no Creator other than He.
4. God is characterised by all the attributes of perfection and is free from all the marks of deficiency; thus He is knowing of all objects of knowledge, is powerful (with power) over all things possible, is willing of all things possible, is speaking, living, hearing and seeing, and He is free from all the attributes of deficiency.
5. God has no similar, no rival, no like, no partner, no helper.
6. God does not inhere in anything else; no originated (thing) subsists in His essence; He is not united with anything else.

7. God is not a substance nor an accident nor a body.
8. (God) is not in any place or in any direction; and He may not be pointed to as being here or there.
9. Movement and change of position may not be predicated of (God).
10. God is seen by the believers of the day of resurrection but without being opposite (to them) or confronting (them) or (being in any) direction (from them).
11. What God willed came to be, and what He did not will did not come to be. Unbelief and sins (in human beings) are by (God's) creating and by His willing but not with His approval.
12. God is rich (and independent);[3] He has no need of anything.
13. There is no judge over (God); and nothing is obligatory for Him, neither (showing) grace, nor (doing what is) the best, nor indemnifying for sufferings, nor rewarding (for obedience), nor punishing for sin. On the contrary, if He rewards, it is by His free gift, and if He punishes, it is by His justice. From Him is nothing bad; and in respect of what He does or what He judges, neither evil nor injustice is predicated of Him. He does what He wills, and judges as He pleases. His activity has no aim[4] (moving Him to act). (It is He who) administers judgement with regard to what He has created and commanded, (but He does so) out of free grace and mercy. There is no judge except Him. Reason has no (power of) judging what things are good and what bad, and whether an action is an occasion for reward or for punishment. The good is what revelation declares good; the bad is what revelation declares bad. The (human) act has no quality, real or relative, in relation to which it is good or bad. Otherwise the matter would be otherwise.
14. God is not divided into parts or portions. He has no limit and no end; His attributes are one by essence, but infinite in respect of what is connected with them (such as objects of knowledge and will). What actually exists of the objects of (God's) power are few out of many; it is for Him to make increases or decreases in respect of what He has created.
15. God has angels possessing wings, twos, threes, fours. Of them are Jibrīl, Mīkā'īl, Isrāfīl, 'Izrā'īl. each one of them has a place well-known. They do not disobey God in what He commands them but do what they are commanded.[5]
16. The Qur'ān is the Speech of God, uncreated. It is written in the copies, recited by the tongues, and remembered in the breasts; what is written is other than the writing, what is recited is other than the reciting and what is remembered is other than the remembering.
17. The names of God are by prescription.

18. The Return (to life) is a reality; the bodies will be gathered together, and the spirits will be restored to them; and in this (state) there will be the requital and the settling of accounts. The Bridge (or Path) is a reality; the Balance is a reality; and the creation (already) of Paradise and Hell.
19. Everlastingly abiding in Paradise are the people of Paradise, and in Hell the unbeliever. The Muslim who has committed a great sin does not abide everlastingly in Hell, but finally goes to Paradise. The forgiving of small and great sins without repentance is possible (for God). Intercession is a reality in the case of those to whom the Merciful has granted it. The intercession of the Messenger of God is for those of his community who have (committed) great sins; he intercedes on their behalf and his request is not refused.
20. The punishment of the tomb is a reality; the interrogation by Munkar and Nakīr is a reality.
21. The sending of messengers (by God), from Adam to our prophet, with evidentiary-miracles (to confirm their claims) is a reality. Muḥammad is the seal of the prophets; there is no prophet after him. The prophets are preserved from sin; they are superior to the higher angels, and the generality of men are superior to the generality of angels.
22. The men of the Pledge of Good Pleasure[6] and the men of Badr are of the people of Paradise.
23. The wonder-miracles of the saints are a reality; thereby God honours whom He wills and marks out by His mercy whom He pleases.
24. The Imām after the Prophet was Abū-Bakr al-Ṣiddīq; his imāmate was by consensus, as the Messenger of God did not nominate anyone (as imām). Then came ʿUmar al-Fārūq, then ʿUthmān Dhū Nūrayn, then ʿAlī al-Murtaḍā; (their) excellence is in this order; the meaning of excellence is that one has a greater reward from God, not that one has more knowledge or is of nobler birth (or the like).
25. Unbelief is the absence of faith. We do not declare any of the people of the Qibla an unbeliever except where he denies the Maker who is (all-)powerful, (effectively) willing and (all-)knowing, or (where he) associates (others with God), or rejects the prophethood (of Muḥammad), or rejects (the evidence) by which the coming of Muḥammad is necessarily known, or rejects a matter on which there has been definite agreement, such as the five pillars of Islam, or considers forbidden (things) permitted. In respect of (doctrines) other than these, he who holds them is a

heretic but not an unbeliever; one (such heretical doctrine) is the (attribution of) corporeality (to God).

26. Repentance is obligatory, but (for God) the acceptance of it is (a matter) of grace and not of obligation.

27. The enjoining of what is right is in accordance with (the character of) what is commanded; thus if what is commanded is obligatory, (the enjoining of it) is obligatory, while if it is laudable, (the enjoining) is laudable. The condition (of it being obligatory or laudable to enjoin what is right) is that it should not lead to strife and that compliance (with the injunction) should be thought probable. Prying curiosity is not permitted.[7]

May God establish you in these sound doctrines, and grant that you do what He loves and approves.

NOTES

1 The 'People of the Sunna and the Community' (*jamāʿa*) is here roughly equivalent to the Sunnites.

2 'Revelation' here translates *sharʿ*.

3 There is a close connection in Arabic between the ideas of 'rich' and 'independent'. The wealthy person is free from want and thus independent and self-sufficient.

4 It seems strange that God should be said to have no aims. The point seems to be that for a human being an aim is something hoped for but not yet realised, and this is inappropriate for God. A similar view is found in Sanūsī, §29, but this teaching is contradicted in Ḥillī, 'God's Justice', §4.

5 In Muslim belief, Gabriel (Jibrīl) is the angel who brought the Qur'ān to Muḥammad, and Michael (Mīkā'īl) is associated with him. Isrāfīl is the angel of resurrection, but is also said to have brought some form of inspiration to Muḥammad before Gabriel brought the Qur'ān. ʿIzrāʾīl is the angel of death.

6 The Pledge of Good Pleasure refers to an incident during the expedition of al-Ḥudaybiya in 6 AH when the situation looked critical for the Muslims. It is variously described as a pledge to fight to the death, or not to flee, or to do whatever Muḥammad ordered. It was thought that entry to Paradise was guaranteed by having taken this pledge, or merely by having fought at the battle of Badr.

7 It was held to be incumbent on all Muslims to enjoin or command what is right and to forbid what is wrong (*al-amr bi-'l-maʿrūf wa-'l-nahy ʿan al-munkar*), that is, to try to ensure that other people did right and avoided wrong, but there were discussions about how this was to be carried out in actual practice. See also Ḥillī, 'The Imāmate', §2 and note.

Al-Sanūsī

Abū ʿAbd Allāh Muḥammad ibn Yūsuf al-Sanūsī (d. 1486 or 1490) was born in Tlemsen and spent most of his life there after studying in Algiers. He is reckoned an Ashʿarite in theology, and was also interested in Ṣūfism. The creed here translated, commonly known as al-Sanūsiyya, was widely known in North and West Africa. The translation is based on the text reproduced in the margin of the Commentary on the creed by al-Bājūrī (d. 1860) in an Egyptian edition dated 1343/1924. Headings have been added to show the structure of the creed. The interest in philosophy is obvious.

In the name of God, the Merciful, the Compassionate! Praise belongs to God. Blessings and peace upon the Messenger of God.

INTRODUCTION

1. Rational judgement comprises three parts: necessity, impossibility and possibility. The necessary is that whose non-existence cannot be conceived in the reason. The impossible is that whose existence cannot be conceived in the reason. The possible is that whose existence and non-existence are both acceptable to the reason.
2. It is necessary according to revelation that every mature believer should know in regard to our Patron what is necessary, what is impossible and what is possible. It is likewise necessary that he should have similar knowledge in respect of the Messengers.

GOD

The Necessary

3. What is necessary in respect God of comprises twenty attributes. (The first six are:) (i) existence; (ii) being from eternity; (iii) being to eternity; (iv) His otherness from originated things; (v) His self-subsistence, that is, His having no need of a substrate or of a determinant; (vi) His uniqueness, that is, (the fact that) there is no second to Him, (either) in respect of His essence or of His attributes or of His acts. Of these six attributes the first, existence, pertains to the self, while the other five are negative.
4. Next there are necessary for Him seven attributes called 'attributes

of forms', namely, (vii) power and (viii) will, which both relate to all actually possible things; (ix) knowledge, which relates to all necessary, possible and and impossible things; (x) life, which does not relate to anything; (xi) hearing and (xii) sight, which both relate to all existents; and (xiii) speech, which is without letter or sound and relates to everything to which knowledge relates.

5. Next there are seven attributes called 'attributes pertaining to forms',[1] inseparable from the previous seven, namely: (xiv-xx) His being powerful, willing, knowing, living, hearing, seeing, speaking.

The Impossible

6. What is impossible in respect of God are twenty attributes, the opposites of the first twenty. (The first are:) (i) non-existence; (ii) having an origin in time; (iii) passing into non-existence; (iv) resemblance to originated things, (either) by His being a body, that is, by His high essence taking a finite part of the void, or by being an accident subsisting in a body, or by being in some direction in respect of body, or by Himself possessing direction, or by being bound to a place or time, or by having His high essence characterised by originated (qualities), or by being characterised by smallness or greatness, or by being characterised by aims in His acts and judgements.
7. Likewise it is impossible for Him to be other than (v) self-subsistent, (either) by being an attribute subsistent in a substrate, or by requiring a determinant.
8. Likewise it is impossible for Him not to be (vi) one, (either) by being composite in His essence, or because there is something which resembles Him in respect of His essence or of His attributes, or because in existence along with Him there is something possessing causal efficacy.
9. Likewise it is impossible that He should be (vii) impotent with regard to anything actually possible; or (viii) that anything in the world should be brought to exist, while He does not will its existence, that is, in the absence of His will for it, or when He is forgetful or neglectful, or through the causal (activity of things) or their natural (workings). Likewise impossible for Him is (ix) ignorance, or what amounts to that, about anything whatever, and also (x) death, (xi) deafness, (xii) blindness, and (xiii) dumbness. The opposites of the attributes pertaining to forms (xiv-xx) are obvious from these.

The Possible

10. What is possible in respect of God is the doing or leaving undone of every actually possible act.

Proofs

11. The proof of God's existence (i) is the originated character of the world, since, if the world had no originator but originated of itself, that would imply that of two equal things[2] one, though equal to the other, should yet preponderate over it without a cause; and that is impossible. The proof of the originated character of the world is that it is inseparable from originated accidents, like movement, rest and so on. What is inseparable from an originated thing is itself originated. The proof of the originated character of the accidents is the observation of their changing from non-existence to existence and from existence to non-existence.
12. The proof that being from eternity (ii) is necessary for God is that, if He did not exist from eternity, then He would be originated, and so would require an originator, and this would imply a vicious circle or an infinite regress.[3]
13. The proof that being to eternity (iii) is necessary for God is that, if it were actually possible that non-existence should be attached to Him, then being from eternity would be denied of Him, for His existence would then be possible and not necessary, and the existence of what is possible can only be originated. But how can that be, seeing that the necessity of God's being from eternity has just been proved?
14. The proof of the necessity of God's otherness (iv) from originated things is that, if He resembled any of them, He would like them be originated; and that is impossible.
15. The proof of the necessity of God's self-subsistence (v) is this. If God required a substrate, then He would be an attribute, and no attribute is characterised (either) by attributes of forms or by attributes pertaining to forms. Our Patron is necessarily characterised by attributes of these two types; therefore He is not an attribute. Again, if He required a determinant, He would be originated. But how can that be, seeing that the proof has already been given of the necessity of His being from eternity and His being to eternity?
16. The proof of the necessity of the uniqueness (vi) of God is this. If he is not unique, it would be implied that nothing of the world exists; (that is) because of the implication of His impotence where He is not unique.

17. The proof of the necessity of God being characterised by power (or omnipotence), will, knowledge and life (vii-x) is that, if any of these was absent from Him, then none of the originated things would exist.
18. The proof of the necessity of God having hearing, sight and speech (xi-xiii) is Scripture, Sunna and consensus. Moreover, if He is not characterised by these, it would be implied that He is characterised by their opposites; but these (opposites) are defects, and in respect of God deficiency is impossible.
19. The proof that the doing of things actually possible or the leaving of them undone is possible for God is that, if any of them were rationally necessary for God or rationally impossible, then the actually possible would have been turned into (either) the necessary or the impossible; and that is contrary to reason.

THE MESSENGERS

The Necessary, the Impossible and the Possible

20. As for the Messengers (of God), there is necessary for them: (i) truthfulness, (ii) trustworthiness, and (iii) the communicating of what they were ordered to communicate to people.
21. Impossible for them are the opposites of these attributes, namely: (i) lying; (ii) disloyalty (or treachery) by doing something (either) strictly forbidden (by God) or disapproved of (by Him); and (iii) the concealing of anything they have been ordered to communicate to people.
22. Possible for them is (the experiencing of) those human accidents, such as illness and the like, which do not lead to any deficiency in their high station.

Proofs

23. The proof of the necessity of their truthfulness (i) is that, if they did not speak truth, it would be implied that God was lying in His report of how He asserted their truthfulness; (this He did) by the evidentiary miracle which was tantamount to His saying, My servant has spoken truly in all his communications from Me.
24. The proof of the necessity of their trustworthiness (ii) is that, if they acted disloyally by doing (either) what is strictly forbidden or disapproved of, then what is forbidden or disapproved of would be turned into (an act of) obedience in their case, because God has commanded us to imitate them in what they say and do, and God does not command the doing of what is forbidden or disapproved of. This very (argument) is also the proof of the necessity of the third (attribute).

25. The proof of the possibility of human accidents happening to them (iv) is the observing of these actually happening to the Messengers. (This may come about) either to increase their reward, or to give a rule (to other people), or to draw (people) away from (worldly things), or to show (people) how little value these have in the sight of God, and that He does not approve of them by way of reward for His prophets and saints in respect of what they have experienced of such (accidents).

The Shahāda

26. The (essential) meanings of all these articles of belief are brought together in the words, 'There is no deity except God; Muḥammad is the Messenger of God'.
27. (This is because) the meaning of Divinity is the independence of the Divine from everything apart from Himself and the need for Him that everything apart from Him has; and the meaning of 'There is no deity except God' is that except God there is nothing (which is) independent of everything apart from itself and (which is) needed by everything other than itself.
28. God's independence of everything apart from Himself necessitates for Him: existence, being from eternity, being to eternity, otherness from originated beings, self-subsistence and exemption from defects. There is also included in (independence) the necessity that God should have hearing, sight and speech. If (all) these attributes were not necessary for Him, He would require an originator or a substrate or someone to keep defects from Him.
29. There is further derived from that (independence) the exemption from having aims in His acts and judgements. Otherwise it would be implied that He is in need of what will achieve His aim. How can that be, seeing that He in His wealth is independent of all apart from Himself?
30. From that (independence) also it is derived that there is no necessity for God (either) to do any of the things actually possible or to leave any undone. If any of these things, such as giving a reward, was rationally necessary for Him, then He would be in need of that thing in order to realise His aim perfectly; for, in respect of God, nothing is necessary except what is perfection for Him. How (can there be such a necessity of acting) seeing that He in His wealth is independent of all apart from Himself?
31. The need for Him of everything apart from Him necessitates that God should have life and all of (the attributes of) power, will and knowledge. If any of these were absent from Him, it would not be actually possible that any of the originated things should exist,

and nothing would be in need of Him. How can that be, seeing that He is the one of Whom all apart from Him are in need?

32. This (need of all for Him) also necessitates that God should be unique; for, if along with Him there was a Second in Divinity, nothing would be in need of Him, since the impotence of both would then be implied. How can that be, seeing that He is the one of whom all apart from Him are in need?
33. Also derived from that (need of all for Him) is the originated character of the world in its entirety, since, if anything of it was from eternity, that thing would be independent of God. How can that be, seeing that He is the one of whom necessarily all apart from Him are in need?
34. Also derived from that (need) is the (assertion) that no entity has any causal efficacy in (producing) any result. Otherwise it would be implied that that result is independent of our Patron. How can that be, seeing that He is the one of whom all apart from Him are in need, altogether and in every instance?
35. This is the case if you suppose that an entity has causal efficacy by its nature. But if you suppose that it has this efficacy by a power that God has made in it, as many ignorant people imagine, then that is impossible also, since then our Patron in bringing into existence certain acts would be in need of a means; and that is false in view of what you know of His necessarily being independent of everything apart from Himself.[4]
36. It has now become clear to you that the words 'There is no deity except God' include the three parts of what it is necessary for the mature believer to know in respect of our Patron. These (three) are: what is necessary in respect of God, what is impossible and what is possible.
37. When we say 'Muḥammad is the Messenger of God', that includes belief in the other prophets and in the angels and in the heavenly books and the Last Day, since Muḥammad came confirming the truth of all that.
38. From this is derived the necessity of the truthfulness of the Messengers and the impossibility for them of lying. Otherwise they would not be trustworthy messengers from our Patron who knows things secret.
39. There is derived also the impossibility of (their) doing (any of) all things to be abstained from, because they are sent to teach people by their words and deeds and silence. It is implied that in all those (words and deeds) there is nothing contrary to the command of our Patron, who chose them (the prophets) above all His creatures and entrusted them with the secret of His inspiration.

40. Again there is derived form that (clause) the possibility of human accidents befalling them, since that does not impair their character of messenger and their high station with God; on the contrary, these help to raise that.
41. It has thus become clear to you how the two clauses of the Shahāda, although they contain only a few letters, include all the articles of belief that it is necessary for a mature believer to know, both in respect of God and in respect of His Messengers. (They achieve this) by combining brevity and comprehensiveness, as we have explained.
42. Revelation has made it (the Shahāda) an expression of the Islam there is in the heart; and no-one's belief is acceptable except in it. The reasonable person, then, should remember it frequently, while bringing to mind the articles of belief it contains, so that these and their meaning are mingled with his flesh and his blood; for, if God will, he will see in them an infinity of secrets and wonders.

CONCLUSION

Now from God is succour. There is no Lord except Him, and no deity apart form Him. We ask Him that He would make us and our loved ones at death to utter the words of the Shahāda, knowing its meaning.

God bless our prince Muḥammad as often as the mindful remember him and the heedless fail to remember him.

God be pleased with all the Companions of the Messenger of God and with those who follow after them in good works until the Day of Judgement.

Peace be upon the Messengers. Praise belongs to the Lord of the Worlds.

NOTES

1 It is not clear why a distinction is made between 'attributes of forms' and 'attributes pertaining to forms' (*ṣifāt al-ma'ānī, ṣifāt ma'nawiyya*); the former are expressed by nouns, the latter by adjectives. The word *ma'nā*, here translated 'form', often has the sense of 'meaning'. It is also not clear what the precise difference is between *mumkināt* and *jā'izāt*, both of which mean 'possible'; perhaps the objects of God's power and will are actually and physically possible, whereas the objects of knowledge are theoretically possible. To show that different words are being used, 'actually possible' is used to translate *mumkināt*.

2 The argument here is somewhat mysterious until it is realised that the two equal things are existence and non-existence. If the world originated of itself, this would mean that existence had preponderated over non-existence without any cause.

3 The standard logical fallacies of vicious circles (*dawr*) and infinite regress (*tasalsul*) are apparently sufficiently well-known to require no explanation. Cf. Ḥillī, 'What is necessarily existent in itself', and 'The Imāmate', §2.

4 This appears to be a denial of the view found in several earlier creeds that God brings about human acts by creating an acting-power (*istiṭā'a*) in the agent.

ʿAllāma-i-Ḥillī

ʿAllāma-i-Ḥillī, the sage of Ḥilla (1250-1325), was born at Ḥilla, an important Shīʿite centre near Baghdad, but later moved to Iran, where he converted the Il-Khānid ruler Öljeytü to Imāmite Shīʿism. The creed here translated is now widely recognised by Imāmites, and is therefore a suitable presentation of their position. Apart from the distinctive doctrine of the imāmate, its position approaches that of the Muʿtazilites at various points. Since no Arabic text was accessible, the translation here is a revision of that in *Al-Bābu 'l-Ḥādī 'Ashar*, translated by W. McE. Miller, London, Royal Asiatic Society, 1928. Miller's translation keeps closely to the Arabic order of words and is sometimes barely comprehensible, especially as the text itself is very succinct and assumes much background knowledge. Fortunately, the main Arabic technical terms have been included either in the translation of the creed or in that of the accompanying commentary.

WHAT IS NECESSARY FOR ALL MATURE BELIEVERS REGARDING KNOWLEDGE OF THE PRINCIPLES OF RELIGION

The scholars all agree in considering obligatory the knowledge of God, of His positive and negative attributes, of what is essential to Him and of what is impossible for Him; and (also the knowledge) of prophethood, of the imāmate and of the Return. All this is (known) by proof, not by following an authority. There must be mention of those things of which it is not possible for any Muslim to be ignorant, since whoever is ignorant of any of them is outside the circle of believers and worthy of eternal punishment.

What is necessarily existent in itself

We say of every object of thought that its existence is either necessary in itself or is possible in itself or is impossible in itself. There is no doubt that here (in the universe) there is something which necessarily exists. If this (thing) is the Necessary-in-itself, then that is what we seek. If, however, this (necessarily existent) is (something) possible, then it would need a cause of existence to cause it to exist necessarily. Now (on the one hand) if this cause of existence is the Necessary-in-itself, that is what we seek; but (on the other hand) if it is something possible, then it would need another cause of existence. In the first case there is a vicious circle, which is a (logical) fallacy. (In the second case) where the cause is another possible (thing), there is an infinite regress (or chain), which is also a (logical) fallacy,[1] for all the links in this chain must be things possible, and therefore share in the impossibility of existing of themselves. They need a cause of existence which must be beyond themselves, and this is the Necessary, which is what we seek.

God's positive attributes, which are eight

1. God is powerful and freely-acting.[2] The world is originated, because it is a body, and every body is inseparable from originated (things), namely, movement and rest. Both these are originated, because both require something preceding them. What is inseparable from originated (things) must itself be originated. It follows (from the world's being originated) that it has a mover, namely God, the powerful and freely-acting. If the cause (of the world) was a (mechanical) cause (and not freely-acting), then necessarily its effect would not continue (to exist) after it (had ceased). That would imply either that the world was eternal (like its cause), or that God (its cause) was originated; and both (these conclusions) are false. God's power is connected with all objects of power. What makes them need His power is (their) possibility. The relation of His essence to all things is equal, and so His power is universal.
2. God is knowing, since His acts are well-ordered and perfect, and everyone who so acts must be knowing. His knowledge is connected with every object of knowledge, because all objects of knowledge are equally related to Him. He is also living, and all living things truly know their objects of knowledge. Thus he must have knowledge, since otherwise He would be lacking something.
3. God is living. Because He is powerful and knowing, he must also be living.
4. God is willing (one who wills) and rejecting (one who wills something should not be). (This is) because the particularising of an act to come about at one time and not another requires a particularising (agency), and that is the will; and also because God gives commands and prohibitions, and these require will for them or against them.
5. God is perceiving, because He is living and therefore truly perceives.[3] This is proved in the Qur'ān, and so it must be asserted that (perception) belongs to Him.
6. God is pre-eternal and existent from eternity, and also everlasting and existent to eternity. (This is) because He is the necessarily

existent. Non-existence, whether prior to existence or following upon existence, is impossible for Him.

7. God is speaking, as all agree. By speech is meant letters and sound which are audible and possess order, and (so) for God to be speaking means that He brings speech into existence in some body. The account given by the Ash'arites is contrary to reason.[4]
8. God is truthful. A lie is necessarily evil, and God is far removed from evil, because it is impossible for him to have any imperfection.

God's negative attributes, which are seven

1. God is not composite. If he were, he would be in need of parts, and what is in need is (only) possible.
2. He is not a body nor an accident nor an atom,[5] because, if He were, He would need a place (that is, would be lacking something); and also because, since a body cannot be separated from originated things, He would be an originated thing, and that is impossible. He cannot be in a place, for then He would be in need of it; nor in a direction, for then He would be in need of it. Likewise, pleasure and pain are not ascribed to Him, because He cannot have a (bodily) constitution. He does not unite with what is other than Himself, because uniting is altogether impossible for Him.
3. God is not a locus for originated things (sc. accidents), because he cannot be acted upon by anything other and cannot have any imperfection.
4. The vision (or seeing) of God is impossible. (This is) because everything that is seen is in a direction (from the viewer); it is either opposite to him or in a comparable relation. If God were seen, He would be a body, which is impossible. In God's word to Moses, 'You shall not see Me' (7.143), the negative (*lan*) is eternal.[6]
5. God has no partner. (This is) because of tradition, and (also) because (if there were a partner), the two would be in conflict with one another, and the orderly existence (of the created world) would be destroyed. (It is also) because He would then have to be composite, since two beings sharing necessary existence would (each) require something to distinguish them.
6. God has no forms or states.[7] (This is because) if His being powerful were due to His power, and His being knowing were due to His knowledge, and so on, He would have need of that form (power, etc.) among His attributes, and His existence would only be possible.
7. God is independent and not in need. (This is) because His being necessarily existent apart from anything else requires His having no need of anything else, whereas all other things are in need of Him.

God's Justice

1. Reason necessarily judges what actions are good, such as returning something entrusted (to one), treating kindly, and truthfulness which is profitable, and also (judges) what actions are bad, such as injustice and a harmful lie. Those who deny all systems of revelation, like the Malāḥida and the philosophers of India, judge good and bad in this way (by reason). Moreover, if (good and evil) are not affirmed by reason, they would be denied by tradition, because the evil of lying would not be affirmed in the case of the author of revelation.[8]
2. We act by choice. This must be so because (1) there is a necessary difference between a person falling from a roof and going down from it by a ladder; otherwise the imposing of duties on us would be impossible and there would be no sin. (It must also be so) because (2) of the evil of God's creating an act in us and then punishing us for it; and (3) because of tradition.
3. It is impossible that God should do evil, because the knowledge he has of evil holds Him back from it. Also He has no motive for doing evil, since the motive would be either need, which is (something) He cannot have, or else the wisdom (of the evil act) which does not exist. Moreover, if it were possible for evil to proceed from God, the proof of revelation to prophets would be impossible. (It may also be said that) the will to do evil is impossible for God, because (such a will) is itself evil.
4. God acts with an aim.[9] (This is because) the Qur'ān teaches this, and also because to deny this would imply (that the act) is vain; and that is evil. The aim of God is not to harm the person but to benefit him. For this (reason) there must be an imposition of duties; and this is the commissioning by God, obliging (persons) to engage firstly and knowingly in (acts) involving labour. (If there were no imposition of duties) God would be inciting to evil by creating (in people) the passions and the desire for evil and hatred of good; (to counter these) there must be a restraint, and that is the imposition of duties. Knowledge (?of blame and praise) is not sufficient because it is easy (to bear) the blame (incurred) in attaining a desired object. The imposition of duties is good, because it makes (people) aware of reward, which is deserved benefit joined with being honoured and respected. This (reward) is impossible without a previous (imposition of duties).
5. Kindness is incumbent on God. Kindness (or favour) is what leads the creature towards obedience and keeps him from disobedience. It is not an aspect of empowering (him) and does not go so far as

compelling (him). The aim (of God) in imposing duties is based on (kindness). If God, in willing an act from (a person), knows that he will not do it without the help of an act which (He), the Willer, can perform easily, then, if God does not perform it, He would be contradicting His own aim; and reason declares this to be evil.

6. An act compensating[10] for the sufferings which come to a person from God is incumbent on Him. A compensatory (act) is a deserved benefit, but without (the person) being honoured and respected (as is the case with reward); otherwise it would be unjust, and God is exalted above that. The compensation must also be in excess of the suffering, since otherwise it would be in vain.

Prophethood

The prophet is a person who brings a message from God without the mediation of any human being.

1. The prophethood of our Prophet, Muḥammad ibn ʿAbd-Allāh ibn ʿAbd-al-Muṭṭalib, the Messenger of God, (is proved) by evidentiary miracles performed by his hand, such as the Qur'ān, the splitting of the moon, the issuing of water from between his fingers, the feeding of a great multitude with a little food, and the praising of God by pebbles in his hand. His evidentiary miracles were more than can be numbered (and prove) his claim to be a prophet. Also, he is truthful, since (falsity) in the duties imposed on people would be evil; and that is impossible.
2. He was immune from sin. Immunity from sin is a hidden kindness shown by God to him on whom He has laid this task (of prophethood), so that he may have no incentive to forsake obedience and commit sin, even though he has the power to do so. Apart from (such immunity), one could have no confidence in the prophet's word, and his prophetic mission would be worthless; and that is impossible.
3. He was immune from sin from the beginning of his life to the end of it, because people's hearts would not be bound to obey one in whose past life various great and small sins and (other) hateful things had been observed.
4. The prophet must be the most excellent of the people of his time. Both reason and tradition declare it evil for an inferior to have precedence over a better (person).
5. The prophet must be far removed from having any baseness in his male ancestry or debauchery in his female ancestry. He must be free from all defects and flaws in his created nature, for this would be imperfection, and he would lose the place in people's hearts that is wanted.

The Imāmate

1. The imāmate is the position of head in religious and worldly matters as deputy (or agent) of the Prophet. Reason shows its necessity. The imāmate is a kindness from God, for, when people have a head and a true guide whom they obey, who avenges the oppressed on the oppressor, and restrains the oppressor from oppressing, then they are in a healthy condition not an unsound one. It was shown above that kindness is incumbent on God.
2. The imām must be immune from sin. Otherwise there would be an infinite regress. An imām is needed for the restraining of the oppressor from oppressing and the avenging of the oppressed on the oppressor; but, if the imām were not immune from sin another imām would be needed (to correct him), and this would lead to an infinite regress, which is impossible. Also, if the imām committed a sin and people had to disapprove of him (because of this), he would lose his place in their hearts, and his position (as head) would be worthless. Again, if the imām were not immune from sin, (the duty of ordinary Muslims) of commanding the good and forbidding[11] the evil would lapse, and that is impossible. Moreover, as guardian of the law the imām must be immune from sin, so that the law is preserved from addition or deletion. God said (referring to possible leaders): 'My covenant does not include the evildoers' (2.118).
3. The imām must be designated. Immunity from sin is in the heart and only God sees it; and so the designation of the imām must be made by someone who knows he has this immunity, or he must bring about an evidentiary miracle to prove his truthfulness.
4. The imām must be the most excellent of the people, because of what has been said above about the prophet.
5. The imām after the Messenger of God is 'Alī ibn Abī-Ṭālib. His designation by the Prophet is found in widely-transmitted reports. He was the most excellent of the people of his time according to God's word, 'ourselves and yourselves' (3.61); and the Prophet needed him in the mutual cursing.[12] Further, since the imām must be immune from sin, and by general agreement no other claimant of the imāmate was immune from sin, 'Alī is the imām. 'Alī is also the most knowing, for the Companions consulted him about their problems but he did not consult any of them; the Prophet said, 'Alī is the best judge of you all', and judgement requires knowledge. Finally, 'Alī is more ascetic than anyone else and divorced the world three times. The proofs of 'Alī's imāmate are innumerable.

The imāms after 'Alī were (in succession): his son al-Ḥasan, then al-Ḥusayn, then ʿAlī ibn al-Ḥusayn then Muḥammad ibn ʿAlī al-Bāqir, then Jaʿfar ibn Muḥammad al-Ṣādiq, then Mūsā ibn Jaʿfar al-Kāẓim, then ʿAlī ibn Musā al-Riḍā, then Muḥammad ibn ʿAlī al-Jawād, then ʿAlī ibn Muḥammad al-Hādī, then al-Ḥasan ibn ʿAlī al-ʿAskarī, then Muḥammad ibn al-Ḥasan, the Lord of the Age. (They are imāms) because each designated his successor, and because of the preceding proofs.

Eschatology

The Muslims are agreed that there must be a bodily return. If there were no return, the imposition of duties would be evil. It is possible (according to reason), and, since the Truthful One (Muḥammad) has said that it is certain, it is real. There are verses which teach this and deny him who rejects it.

The resurrection of all to whom compensation must be given or who must give compensation is necessary by reason. The return of all others is necessary by tradition.

All that the Prophet taught must be acknowledged, namely, the Bridge, the Balance, the speaking of the members (of the body), and the opening of the books.[13] These things are possible, and the Truthful One has informed us of them, and so they must be acknowledged.

Also there are reward and punishment. The explanation of these which has been transmitted is based on revelation.

The commanding of good and forbidding of evil (is incumbent on each Muslim), provided that in doing so he knows what is good and what is evil. This applies to what has yet to happen, because to command or forbid what is past is nonsense. (The benefit envisaged) should have some (good) effect and not to damage.

NOTES

1 The logical fallacies mentioned here, vicious circle and infinite regress (the latter also in 'The Imāmate', §2), also occur in Al-Sanūsī, §12.

2 The combination of freely-acting (*mukhtār*) with powerful as an attribute of God is surprising. It seems to point to a contrast with the mechanical or physical cause (*mūjib*); but the background of thought behind all this is not obvious.

3 What Sunnites keep separate as hearing and seeing are here united under the term 'perceiving' (*mudrik*).

4 What is here called the Ashʿarite view is that of all mainstream Sunnites.

5 'Atom' here translates *jawhar*, but it is not stated how it differs from 'body' (*jism*).

6 This differs from the Sunnite view that God will be seen in Paradise.

7 It is not clear what is meant by 'forms' (*maʿānī*) and 'states' (*aḥwāl*). Since the creed has spoken of God's knowledge, it perhaps means that attributes such as this have no hypostatic quality.

8 The word *shar'* here must mean revelation in general and is not restricted to legal matters; cf. *Muhammad's Mecca*, p. 64. Malāḥida is the plural of *mulḥid*, which can mean 'heretic', but probably means 'atheist' here, though without any precise reference.

9 This contrasts with the view of some later Sunnites that God has no aim. Miller does not seem to have understood the article properly, for he translates *ba'th* as 'responsibility'. The word is used for the commissioning of a prophet, and so is here translated as 'commissioning' in the sense that God calls on the ordinary Muslim to fulfil the law, and so to accept a degree of responsibility.

10 The ideas about compensation here and in §7 appear to be peculiar to Shī'ism.

11 The duty of commanding the good and forbidding the evil (*al-amr bi-'l-ma 'rūf wa-'l-naḥy 'an al-munkar*) is a duty of ordinary Muslims (and not specially of the imām, as Miller seems to have thought); cf. §7 and Ījī, §27. Henri Laoust wrote about it as follows:

> The Muslim community is ... the community of the just mean, that which 'enjoins the good and forbids the evil' (*al-amr* ...). Each member of the community is bound to correct all that, in his sphere of influence, appears to him contrary to the Law, by his effective action if he can, by a verbal admonition where he cannot (act), and lastly by the firm intentions of his heart. (*Ibn Taimīya*, p. 255)

12 The 'mutual cursing' (*mubāhala*) refers to events associated with the Qur'ānic verse 3.61. This says that, if someone disputes with Muḥammad about the knowledge which has come to him (from God) about Jesus, each is to call down the curse of God on himself and his family if they are lying. This was thought to be effective. Muḥammad is said to have challenged a deputation of Christians to this mutual cursing, and to have had with himself 'Alī, Fāṭima and their children al-Ḥasan and al-Ḥusayn.

'Alī's divorcing of the world refers to a story about him. The world is said to have come to him in the form of a beautiful girl, and then he is said to have pronounced the threefold formula of divorce.

13 'The opening of the books' has here been substituted for Miller's 'flying of the books'. The latter would seem to be due to an error in the text, since there appears to be no reference to such a phenomenon in any standard work.

Index

ISLAMIC CREEDS
A SELECTION

TRANSLATED BY
W. MONTGOMERY WATT

There are no official creeds in Islam comparable to the Apostles' creed and the Nicene creed in Christianity. In mainstream Sunnite Islam, however, there is broad agreement about the chief doctrines, and over the centuries these have been expressed in creeds by individuals and gourps, some of which have been widely recognised and used for instruction.

These creeds are basic material for the study of Islamic religion, and a selection is given here in translation, together with a historical introduction, explanatory notes, and a single Shi'ite creed to show the contrast.

William Montgomery Watt is Professor Emeritus of Arabic at Edinburgh Univerity, and author of many works on Islamic history, philosophy and culture, including *Islamic Philosophy and Theology*, *Islamic Political Thought* and, with Richard Bell, *Introduction to the Qur'an*.

Jacket illustration: Maqamat of al-Hariri, Iraq, c.1225

Edinburgh University Press
22 George Square
Edinburgh
EH8 9LF
www.eup.ed.ac.uk